# SONGS OF PRAISE

Andrew Barr

# Songs of Praise

## The Nation's Favourite

A LION BOOK

Published by
**Lion Publishing plc**
Sandy Lane West, Oxford, England
www.lion-publishing.co.uk
ISBN 0 7459 5085 X

By arrangement with the BBC

The BBC logo and the *Songs of Praise* logo are trade
marks of the British Broadcasting Corporation and
are used under licence

BBC logo © BBC 1996
*Songs of Praise* logo © BBC 2000

First edition 2001
10 9 8 7 6 5 4 3 2 1 0

A catalogue record for this book is available
from the British Library

Typeset in 10.5/16 Modern 880
Printed and bound in Singapore

## Acknowledgments

### Pictures
p. 19: copyright © Roger Hutchings; p. 20 (main
picture): reproduced with the permission of the
Liverpool Daily Post and Echo; p. 20 (inset) and
p. 21: copyright © John Forrest; p. 22: copyright
© Liz Ryves-Brown; p. 24 (top): copyright © Roger
Hutchings; p. 25: copyright © Medwyn Hughes/
Martin Neeves Photography; p. 27: copyright ©
Ralph Smith; p. 29: copyright © the *Radio Times*,
reproduced with permission; p. 30 and 31: copyright
© Ralph Smith; p. 33: copyright © Ralph Smith;
p. 34: copyright © Walter McEvoy; p. 37: copyright
© Liz Ryves-Brown; p. 50: copyright © Chris Mann;
p. 56 (left): copyright © Roger Hutchings; p. 65 (left):
copyright © Chris Mann; p. 74: copyright © British
Railways Board; p. 74 (top) and pp. 74–75 (middle):
copyright © Chris Mann; p. 78: copyright © Roger
Hutchings; p. 79: copyright © Chris Mann; p. 88:
Noel Tredinnick; p. 95 (right): copyright © Roger
Hutchings; p. 99 (left): copyright © BBC 2001,
reproduced with permission; p. 100: copyright ©
Medwyn Hughes/Barry C. Evans; p. 107 (main
picture): reproduced with the permission of the
Western Mail; p. 108: copyright © Ralph Smith.

### Text
'Show me the way': words and music by Wendy Craig,
copyright © BMG Music Publishing Ltd. All rights
reserved. Used by permission.

'Jesus, good above all other': words by Percy Dearmer
(1867–1936) from *Enlarged Songs of Praise* by
permission of Oxford University Press.

'Be still, for the presence of the Lord' by David
J. Evans, copyright © 1986 Kingsway's Thankyou
Music, PO Box 75, Eastbourne. Used by permission.

'Seed, scattered and sown' by Dan Feiten, copyright
© 1987 Ekklesia Music, Inc., Denver, Colorado 80222,
PO Box 99267.

Extracts from the Reverend Dr Colin Morris's sermon
in Westminster Abbey on October 1991 are reproduced
by kind permission.

Scripture quotations taken from the *Holy Bible, New
International Version*, copyright © 1973, 1978, 1984
by International Bible Society. Used by permission
of Hodder & Stoughton Limited. All rights reserved.
'NIV' is a registered trademark of International Bible
Society. UK trademark number 1448790.

# CONTENTS

*Acknowledgments*     6

*Foreword*     8

## Introduction
**The Making of a Producer**     10

*One*    ## The Nation's Favourite?
*Songs of Praise* **and its Claim to Fame**     16

*Two*    ## In the Beginning...
**The Birth Pains of** *Songs of Praise*     26

*Three*    ## The Birds Take Over
**The Secret World of** *Songs of Praise* **Technicians**     36

*Four*    ## 'Don't Be the Yorkshire Pudding Choir!'
*Songs of Praise* **in the Making**     44

*Five*    ## Brief Encounters
*Songs of Praise* **Comes Down Your Way**     54

*Six*    ## It'll Be All Right on the Night
**Why** *Songs of Praise* **Has Never Been a Disaster Movie**     63

*Seven*    ## 'Now You'll Only Get This Once...'
**The Stranger Excursions of** *Songs of Praise*     73

*Eight*    ## Calling the Tune
**The Music Makers of** *Songs of Praise*     80

*Nine*    ## One of the Family
**Presenting** *Songs of Praise*     90

*Ten*    ## Harry and Thora
**A Tribute to Two Great Stars**     98

*Eleven*    ## Forty Years On
**A Glimpse of the Future**     104

*Selected* Songs of Praise *presenters and locations: 1961–2001*     110

# Acknowledgments

After making *Songs of Praise* programmes on and off for 30 years, beginning in 1971 and going out on a high in July 2000 with a special royal edition from Glamis Castle, the list of people I have fond memories of is of telephone-directory proportions. Michael Wakelin is the ninth series producer of the 'nation's favourite', and 12 TV producers currently devote most of their working lives to the programme. The roll of presenters must be near the 200 mark. So it is impossible to mention by name here all those who have helped to tell the stories of grief and glory that make *Songs of Praise*.

Morag Reeve of Lion Publishing and Hugh Faupel of BBC Religion have shown great confidence in me – equal to Ray Short's original act of faith in giving an upstart researcher his chance to direct the programme in 1970 – and I am very grateful to them both. I would also like to thank Nick Rous and Jenni Dutton

Songs of Praise at Glamis Castle sends 100th-birthday greetings to Her Majesty Queen Elizabeth, the Queen Mother.

of Lion Publishing for their design and editorial work. Michael Websell from the BBC Written Archives and Judith Sharp, *Songs of Praise*'s production secretary, have helped me with fact-finding, past and present. Kathleen Frew, a good friend and former colleague, has created an orderly manuscript out of disorderly drafts.

Finally, I owe immeasurably much to Liz, my wife: writer, former TV producer and the very first researcher to travel across Britain and find the people whose interviews have made *Songs of Praise* since 1977. No matter that we occasionally fall out over a programme: we survived surely the ultimate test when Liz was producing *Songs of Praise* and Thora Hird's *Praise Be!* for BBC1, while I was producing ITV's *Highway*, presented by Harry Secombe, for transmission on exactly the same day and at the same time. Many scripts for the rival channels emerged at our dining-room table between 1986 and 1991. We were lucky that nobody referred us to the Monopolies Commission.

On the night in May 1984 when the news of Sir John Betjeman's death was announced, Liz and I listened together to an old location tape recording I had made of John. He was being filmed on Tennyson Down in the Isle of Wight; from behind him came the mournful clang of a buoy rocking in the Solent, as from memory he recited one of Tennyson's best-known poems, 'Crossing the Bar', also popular as a hymn:

*Sunset and evening star,*
  *And one clear call for me!*

*And may there be no moaning of the bar,*
  *When I put out to sea,*

*But such a tide as moving seems asleep,*
  *Too full for sound and foam,*
*When that which drew from out the boundless deep*
  *Turns again home.*

*Twilight and evening bell,*
  *And after that the dark!*
*And may there be no sadness of farewell,*
  *When I embark;*

*For tho' from out our bourne of Time and Place,*
  *The flood may bear me far,*
*I hope to see my Pilot face to face,*
  *When I have crost the bar.*

After reciting the last line, that night on the open downs looking across the water into the New Forest, John turned to the camera and said that what made the poem for him was that Tennyson did not *know* that he would see his 'Pilot' – he could only *hope* that it would be so. As Liz and I sat listening – a little tearfully – we recognized the hope that lies at the heart of every *Songs of Praise*.

ANDREW BARR
*April 2001*

# Foreword

In Autumn 2001, *Songs of Praise* celebrates its 40th year on BBC1, making it one of the world's longest-running television programmes. You have to ask yourself, what is it about any programme that keeps it a favourite on prime-time television for four decades, watched now by as many as six million viewers in Britain each Sunday and many millions more around the world?

Without a doubt, *Songs of Praise* is a vital part of Sunday-evening viewing, as dearly loved as a good friend, and yet full of surprises over the years because of its energy and commitment to sharing Christian faith and music through the highest possible standards of television production.

At its heart is congregational singing in churches which vary in size and denomination, but unite in enthusiasm and fellowship. Whole communities rally round when *Songs of Praise* comes to visit, with huge choirs gathering for weeks beforehand to rehearse together so that they can provide the choral backbone of singing 'on the night'

for a congregation drawn from the local area. To sit in a beautifully lit church for a *Songs of Praise* recording, accompanied by first-class musicians and guided by one of the top church-music conductors in Britain, is quite simply an experience people remember for years! Traditional favourites, which echo round huge, historic cathedrals, or joyous choruses that get your toes tapping in a more modern setting, can make the hairs on the back of your neck stand on end. Take it from me! I've been lucky enough to be at more than 200 *Songs of Praise* recordings over my 14 years as a presenter on the programme – and I still love every minute of it!

But *Songs of Praise* is also committed to being wherever people are, which has meant that increasingly we take our celebration out of the church setting and onto the streets, beaches, theatres, concert halls, shopping centres, circus big tops – even football stadiums. Our crowning glory was perhaps the huge marking of the millennium, when

70,000 people raised their voices on a live programme at the new international rugby stadium in Cardiff. Lesley Garrett joined us for the first event ever at the new number-one court at Wimbledon, bringing the 10,000-strong audience to hushed silence as she sang 'The Lord's Prayer'. A choir of 5,000 was accompanied by 1,000 brass instrumentalists, the biggest brass band ever assembled, for Music Live from Leeds, and 1,000 members of Welsh male-voice choirs joined forces for us at the Royal Albert Hall.

All these are wonderful memories of spectacular and moving editions of *Songs of Praise* in Britain, but we've travelled the world too – marking in words and music the last Easter of the millennium where it all began in the Holy Land; filling the Sydney Opera House at the start of the 2000 Olympic Games; sharing with Christians in Hong Kong just before the province was handed back to China; and celebrating Easter in one of the Vatican Basilicas when, during the programme, His Holiness the Pope gave a very special greeting to *Songs of Praise* viewers.

If music is the backbone of *Songs of Praise*, then the people who speak so candidly about their faith in between the hymns are surely its inspiration. They often share with great honesty and generosity the challenges they face in their own lives, and the part that faith plays in their reactions and decisions. We know from the many letters we receive that what they have to say about their own experiences can often bring great comfort and strength to those who watch – and, for that reason, I think *Songs of Praise* is more than 'just television'. It is an act of fellowship shared by millions in a world where, for many, our programme provides the only Christian element in their lives.

For 40 years, we have celebrated Christianity in music, reflecting the life of our country and our world, responding to common concerns and presenting modern-day moral and ethical dilemmas in the light of 2,000 years of faith. It's no wonder that all of us who work on *Songs of Praise* feel a great sense of privilege and pride to be part of a programme which means so much to so many week by week.

PAM RHODES
*April 2001*

# Introduction

## The Making of a Producer

'It's all the fault of you *Songs of Praise* people,' said the man on the door at the parish church. It was my very first involvement with the programme and I was explaining why I was late arriving for the planning meeting – there had been a huge queue when I went to buy stamps at the nearby post office. 'With your BBC vans in the town', he said, 'there's bound to be a long queue for TV licences, before one of your lot goes round knocking on doors!' Now, whether or not the recording vans for *Songs of Praise* do in fact include a TV-detector unit must remain the BBC's secret, but his view was about as plausible as my own had been. I had come to the conclusion that all the town's inhabitants were queuing up to buy licences just so that they could see themselves singing hymns on television.

It was the autumn of 1971. *Songs of Praise* had come to the Lincolnshire Wolds, to St James's Parish Church in the law-abiding and God-fearing town of Louth. I had been to Louth once before, in the 1960s, when working as a sound recordist in a BBC film unit that was making a programme about the poet

Alfred, Lord Tennyson, presented by Sir John Betjeman. John enthused about St James's, and the fact of its having the tallest spire in Britain (by which means Louth announced itself to all travellers in the county that John insisted on calling 'Lincs.'). I remember how we all stopped in our tracks as the spire came into view and the poet, as he did so often in front of a fine church, stood in the street and doffed his battered trilby.

Travelling around Britain filming with John Betjeman over several weeks in the 1960s gave me, I now think, the best insight I could have had for my later understanding of what *Songs of Praise* meant and still means to so many of its viewers. Moreover, the late Poet Laureate's famous love of churches, recorded with a sometimes dotty brilliance in the two-volume *Pocket Guide to English Parish Churches*, was to become my constant companion throughout 30 years of making religious television programmes, including *Songs of Praise*.

While writing about a TV programme that so many millions of people think of as their own, I am haunted by the thought that this book, like *Songs of Praise* itself sometimes, is almost certain to disappoint some people. I am certain to leave out the very ingredient that is 'it' to one reader; to another it will be a quite different 'it' that makes watching *Songs of Praise* the highlight of their week – and I will probably omit that too. However, I persevere, because I too love *Songs of Praise*, and want to share some of the experiences of making a programme that has now been coming into millions of homes Sunday by Sunday for 40 years.

To begin with, I thought this book would more or less write itself, because I had so many recollections from 30 of those 40 years that I thought would interest people, having worked on the programme myself from time to time as a director, a producer and, for a while, an editor. But once I began reminiscing I realized that there were so many hundreds of stories, so many thousands of people in so many hundreds of places, both at home and abroad – who have all been part of the experience – that one book might well not be big enough to contain them all. Talking to past and present producers, directors and presenters, anecdotes and memories began to pile high on top of one another, until I became completely diverted from my original plan and didn't know where to begin and where to end.

I was encouraged, however, by another writer, Richard Morris, author of several books on church architecture, who said that as he reached his last pages he recognized that perhaps 'vestiges of his early intentions' remained.

When *Songs of Praise* began in 1961, we didn't have a television in our family home. Sunday was a day for the wireless and the *Light Programme* and Alan Keith's *Your Hundred*

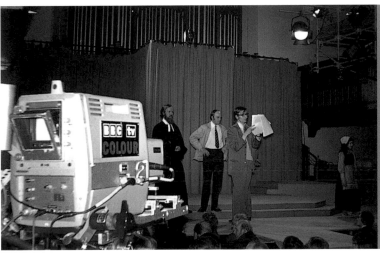

Final rehearsals in St Paul's, Johnstone, in 1972 as Andrew Barr makes sense of his script.

*Best Tunes* were listened to more religiously than *Sunday Half-Hour*. My mother used to sing along with *Sing Something Simple*, and we sometimes celebrated New Year's Eve by inviting an ever-diminishing band of friends and neighbours to sing out the old year with us. My own voice test at school had lasted a matter of seconds before I was rejected for the choir, but I grew up chanting the psalms at my Presbyterian father's side, in St George's, Beckenham. This Anglican church, which was later to host a quite magnificent *Songs of Praise*, was at that time a bit in the doldrums, at least as far as Matins was concerned. My childish prayer to God that the old priest who officiated would not feel too disheartened and lonely with a dwindling choir and congregation was perhaps an unpromising beginning for a future *Songs of Praise* producer.

It was to be vision rather than sound that kindled my own faith, when with thousands of others I queued for hours in 1962 to get my first glimpse of Coventry Cathedral and Graham Sutherland's extraordinary tapestry 'Christ in Glory'. From then on, everything that I could see and hear in the cathedral and everything that happened there gave me the reassuring and uplifting feeling that all would be well. I had always hoped to be an architect, but I couldn't manage the mathematics. If I couldn't design a church, I discovered there that I could at least use a camera and a smuggled-in tape recorder to share the experience I was having – usually with my family and the same long-suffering friends from our New Year's Eve singalongs. Perhaps one day I could even make a programme...

Eight years later, having trained and worked as a BBC sound recordist in the film department, I finally made it into the religious broadcasting department as a researcher. I went along for my first experience of a television team meeting, where producers and directors review the department's work of the past week. Arriving with a head brimming with my own ideas and opinions, I could scarcely wait until we reached *Songs of Praise* on the agenda, because I had watched it attentively at home. 'I could do better than that,' I said.

At first there was silence as everyone looked in surprise at the junior upstart in the room. Then a friendly faced man, who had been sitting quietly smoking a pipe, eyed me across the table. 'OK, matey,' he said finally, with a rather gimlet-eyed look, 'maybe I'll give you a go.' Which, to my amazement and to the amazement of everyone round the table, was exactly what he did. It was the beginning of many years working with the producer of the programme that I had offered to improve, the Reverend Raymond Short. Ray is an endlessly patient, generous-hearted Methodist minister who, although now retired and happier with his watercolour sketchpad than an outside-broadcast unit, is still an excellent teacher who seems to have been born with a natural gift for directing TV cameras.

Louth was a good introduction for a new member of the *Songs of Praise* team. Choirs and congregations from all the local churches had vied for seats in the spacious nave and under the wonderful tower, which John Betjeman described as 'one of the last great medieval Gothic masterpieces'. As people were being quite literally jammed into the pews by the churchwardens, it seemed that we were acting out some lines from *The First Church Warden's Book of Louth*, quoted by John Betjeman in his own *Pocket Guide to English Parish Churches*: 'From the richest to the poorest, all seem to have been affected with a like zeal.' And on this autumn Thursday evening in 1971 everyone in town, it seemed, had to be in St James's Church.

On Ray's instructions, I had come to watch and learn. And I learned a lot that night in Louth. I watched Hazel Lewthwaite, the director, carefully working out each shot with her four huge cameras, to show not only all the singers but also the magnificence of the building. It was not easy, since for the cameras to be able to see and show everyone in the church, huge lamps, attached to masses of scaffolding, were suspended everywhere, and the cameras had to avoid looking at any of them and, above all, at one another. Hazel was doing what we all have to learn to do – creating an illusion that, in spite of a mass of invasive technology and 30 or more technicians hard at work, there is nothing to be seen but a beautiful and holy place filled with God's people singing hymns. Although today's modern cameras need much less bright lighting, fewer heavy lamps and less scaffolding, relating architecture to people is still one of the great challenges for every *Songs of Praise* director. Yet it almost seems sometimes as if the Creator briefed the medieval architects about the need to make a mighty church ready for the technology of 500 years hence. Ancient churches are greatly sympathetic to the camera's eye.

Former series producer Ray Short with his rare *Songs of Praise* trophy, a *Radio Times* cover.

I began that first day to learn to live with the *Songs of Praise* time-shift. Here we were in Louth in October, before harvest thanksgiving, but we were recording Advent hymns for a December broadcast. To plan and complete a major weekly programme, the producers live and work like those Christmas-card producers who must finish their designs before the first week of Lent. Over the years, many congregations have sung carols at a Christmas tree, only to see it vanish again for the four weeks of Advent, or have filled their church with spring flowers for an Easter *Songs of Praise*, only to have to strip the church bare the next day for Lent.

I also discovered at that first recording in Louth why *Songs of Praise* producers never need to diet. The only way to persuade the busy people of Britain to come to church for several hours of rehearsing and recording eight or nine hymns is to arrange for it to happen during the evening. So, after a day or two spent rigging the lights, cameras and sound equipment, BBC crews can be found forlornly wandering the streets of whatever town they are in, trying – often in vain – to find an oasis where hot food

or two and that your camera shots are odd and difficult, a team of technicians can transform the most inexperienced director's peculiar ideas into an effective broadcast.

Ray Short was as good as his word – he did 'give me a go'. After I had watched *Songs of Praise* being made that night in Louth, the next morning Hazel Lewthwaite and Ray sat me down at the vision-mixing desk in the mobile control room parked outside the church. Ray had decided that my best learning experience

Inside the mobile control room as Liz Barr directs cameras for the 21st-anniversary *Songs of Praise* from Wesley's Chapel, London, in 1983.

is served before 6.30 p.m. or after 10 p.m.

I learned a lot very quickly, but it was nothing compared with what I still had left to learn. Programme-making of this sort is a team experience. Even if people disagree with your approach, or think you need taking down a peg

would be to direct the cameras from the same church for the following Sunday's live outside broadcast of choral Holy Communion on BBC1. 'You'll be all right,' said Hazel, when she'd shown me how to work the mixing desk, and set off home saying that she would be watching. 'No mistakes, now,' she added.

After the camera rehearsal Ray dissected my script. 'What's that for?' he kept asking as he puzzled over my 'better' ideas, peering at me over the half-spectacles he called his 'depressed ecclesiasticals'.

First shot of *Songs of Praise* from Eastbourne directed by Andrew Barr in 1974.

Out went one after another of my 'better' – and often meaningless – ideas. But in the end I survived. The rector, Michael Adie (later to become bishop of Guildford), and all the church congregation were patient through the rehearsals, which were really for my benefit, not theirs. Ray chewed his pipe as the programme went out live on the air, disguising what must have been wracked nerves. As it ended he gave me a friendly pat on the shoulder. 'That was all right,' he said. It was, and is still, the height of praise from *Songs of Praise*'s longest serving and most prolific producer.

Going without an evening meal is, of course, a ridiculously tiny sacrifice compared with the effort and enthusiasm of the more than two million singers who have helped make *Songs of Praise* over the last 40 years. Some stalwarts even come back for a second or third time, although they know that they need to timetable in an extra visit to the gym before the recording and a long lie-in afterwards. Making 'the nation's favourite' is seriously hard work. Communities and churches and other *Songs of Praise* recording locations are all crammed with talented people. They may never have appeared on TV before, and perhaps never will again, but they always go to extraordinary lengths, working with the BBC teams to make 'their' programme a success. They are the unsung heroes to whom this book is dedicated. When it goes well it is hugely enjoyable, and as for the programme's producers, they deserve the observation of one of the many volunteers: 'Just think, you've been paid to have fun!'

If you, like the people who have taken part in a programme and watch it going out, can recognize in this book at least something of the sounds and sights and stories of *Songs of Praise* as you know it, I will be relieved.

# The Nation's Favourite?

## *Songs of Praise* and its Claim to Fame

'The nation's favourite'. A familiar phrase, but how can such a large claim be made for a TV programme? It was not a question we – the editorial team from Lion Publishing, Hugh Faupel, the editor of *Songs of Praise*, and I – talked about at length at the original meeting to discuss this book. There was only the shortest of pauses when the title was being pondered before Hugh said, 'It's got to be *Songs of Praise: The Nation's Favourite*, hasn't it?'

Noticing that Hugh was looking out of the window, some of us turned to look out too. There is a spectacular outlook from the top floor of the BBC's new Broadcasting House in Manchester, home of the *Songs of Praise* production team. Both north and south, there are far-reaching views not only of the modern high-tech face of the city, but also of dark, soot-blackened Victorian church spires and factory chimneys, made famous by the artist L.S. Lowry. In the distance lie woodland, fields and then the hills of the Peak District and, further north, the Pennines. It struck me that no matter which part of this vast panorama I looked at, I could hear the sound of choirs singing great hymns from *Songs of Praise* of the past, or imagine a heart-piercing solo from a future Choir Girl of the Year in an edition yet to happen.

Somehow the weekly 35 minutes of television seem to belong naturally and unselfconsciously to the everyday landscape in which we all live. Our decision about the title of this book was mainly influenced by statistics, and the almost astonishing success of a religious programme that is still watched on Sunday evenings all through the year by millions of TV viewers. But I also think, as a former editor of *Songs of Praise* myself, that the view from the BBC Manchester office played its part.

Travelling around to see today's *Songs of Praise* in action and hearing stories of its 40-year history, I have kept the title 'the nation's favourite' on trial. Was it earned when it figured in that addictive ITV spectacular *Who Wants to be a Millionaire?* The poker-faced inquisitor, Chris Tarrant, turned his spotlight on yet another contestant eager to win a million pounds. 'So, for £1,000, what was the soap opera featuring Den and Angie Watts? Was it…' – after he had named three familiar soap titles – '… *Songs of Praise*?' (The contestant won £1,000 without the need to 'phone a friend'.)

The aptness of the title 'the nation's favourite' was called into question when the comedian Rowan Atkinson turned his spotlight on *Songs of Praise*. His *Not the Nine O'Clock News* sketch begins with a deliberately off-pitch version of the signature tune. Then, after a shaky caption over the dullest of empty high streets, Rowan is found in the pulpit as an apparently telly-friendly vicar, welcoming viewers to his church. But he is quickly overcome with rage as he relives the previous week's Sunday evening in his church when, without TV cameras, he worshipped with a congregation of three, which included a dog. 'So where were you miserable telly addicts then?' he asks. He was touching a real nerve.

Many people comment on how full the churches are for *Songs of Praise* – and how bare and bleak

**Left: All Souls', Langham Place, a regular setting for *Songs of Praise*.**

**Above: Christmas *Songs of Praise* from Trafalgar Square.**

on so many other Sunday nights. So perhaps it is not always a favourite with everyone, or at least not with tired clergy, who hear only 'the melancholy, long, withdrawing roar' of the Sea of Faith described by the poet Matthew Arnold, but who nevertheless keep going week after week, saying their evening office in an almost empty church.

When a fictional *Songs of Praise* descended on *The Vicar of Dibley*, giving Geraldine, the woman priest portrayed by Dawn French, the chance to organize a programme, the plot included another familiar thorny ingredient. Who would be picked to be filmed choosing their favourite hymn and who would be the TV star of the front row of the choir? It was funny because it is true. One *Songs of Praise* researcher remembers trying breathlessly to keep up with an energetic vicar bounding around his parish shouting, 'You're in!' at one inhabitant and, 'I didn't see you in church last week, so you're not on my list for *Songs of Praise*!' at another. To everyone he met he yelled, 'I've got the BBC with me, so watch out!'

It can be funny in a sad but understandable way how local rivalries, which may have been simmering for years, come to the boil when *Songs of Praise* comes to town. One extremely formidable organist, after a row about hymn tunes in which she had insisted on having her own way, was subjected to 'heavy-breathing' telephone calls for weeks afterwards. I also remember a fiery priest who cycled around his parish in the dead of night delivering letters of dismissal to choir members and musicians who had incurred his wrath at a *Songs of Praise* rehearsal. While I was editor there was, on one occasion, a demand, as a tabloid daily reported it, for a church to be reconsecrated because

*Songs of Praise* had been recorded there. It appeared that some empty beer cans had been discovered in one of the pews. The finger of suspicion was pointed at the BBC team.

The solution to all these little local difficulties is for the television producer to take all the blame. BBC producers have to understand that, whatever their ambition, *Songs of Praise* is not *their* programme. We are merely visitors to living communities full of talent, scrapping with each other one moment and celebrating together the next. No one involved with making *Songs of Praise* can fail to be moved by the pride, passion and enthusiasm with which local choirs, conductors, organists and congregations take part week by week. While stars such as Daniel O'Donnell or Placido Domingo may have a popular appeal when they make a special guest appearance, the programme really belongs to – and is made by – its viewers. It is the viewers who will leave their homes once or twice in their lives to go along to a recording of *Songs of Praise* to be part of the congregation and be shown singing in close-up.

'What is it that makes watching other people's mouths opening and shutting as they sing *Songs of Praise* so engaging?' asked the distinguished choral conductor Sir David Willcocks, when I was reminding him recently of his many past appearances conducting the programmes. 'Is it not that we know that really, with just a very little help, we can all sing? Perhaps it's just one of those rare moments when we recognize that there are ways of living together in harmony – we can all take part in *Songs of Praise*.'

## The Miniver effect

Hymns seem always to have had a part to play in the background of our lives. People remember and love hymns that they learned at school long after they have stopped going to church. They resonate with something very deep in the human psyche. In the middle of the Second World War, *Mrs Miniver*, a Hollywood film starring Greer Garson and Walter Pidgeon, was released. It was based on a short story written in 1939 by Jan Struther, an English hymn-writer. (Her best-known hymn, 'Lord of all hopefulness', is sometimes sung to a tune called 'Miniver'.) The film portrayed the wartime spirit of an archetypal English family in Kent, and the heroism of the crews of the little ships that sailed to France and rescued the troops from the beaches at Dunkirk. In the final scene the villagers, who have all fallen out over something, gather in their bomb-damaged parish church. The vicar exhorts all those present to forget their differences and fight the real enemy – fight with all God's strength. Then, as one, they all stand to sing 'Onward Christian Soldiers' and, as the familiar words are sung, close-ups of the film's stars show that all the old jealousies and enmities are forgotten. Then,

Sally Magnusson and Placido Domingo prepare for 'Carols from Prague', a festival *Songs of Praise*.

as on many a *Songs of Praise* programme, the camera pans up from the congregation to show the medieval roof – only in this case there's a huge gaping hole where it has been bombed, through which the open sky is visible. The sky fills with RAF fighters taking off to defend Britain. Not a dry eye in the cinema.

It is worth remembering how much films about Britain, its landscape and its music lifted people's spirits in the Second World War. 'Get to it and sing with it,' was the exhortation Herbert Morrison, then minister of home security, told workers. In 1940, the actor Robert Donat said in a broadcast that whenever he felt 'tired and full of doubt' he turned to the 'rationalizing solace and courage of music'.

And even today, *Songs of Praise* – at its best conveying sentiment rather than sentimentality – reminds me of the films made 50 years ago by the great documentary-maker, Humphrey Jennings. In *Listen to Britain*, the sounds of popular BBC radio programmes are cut to shots of town and country at war, while ordinary people at work are depicted as united in the cause of peace. Factory machinists sing together as loudspeakers relay the relentlessly jolly radio programme, *Music While You Work*. It seems uniquely British and I'm not at all surprised that cinema audiences wept in recognition of all the familiar things they were fighting for.

# LIVERPOOL ECHO

The best-selling newspaper on Merseyside

Monday, April 21, 1997

**30p**

# MERSEY GLORY

SONGS PRAISE
MERSEY GLORY

24-page supplement
to celebrate the

## Songs of Prai

*event at*

## Goodison Park

on Sunday, May 4

9 771361 515212

**RSEY GLORY**

1997 and, 'Glory, glory, glory,' it's Mersey Glory as 000 singers fill the stands at Everton Football Club.

*left, inset:* **Each stand has its own conductor to follow** l Leddington-Wright's overall beat.

*low, top:* **Opening fanfare from the King's Division** rmandy Band, conducted by Captain Keith Hatton.

*low, bottom:* **Producer John Forrest's choreography** orks wonders.

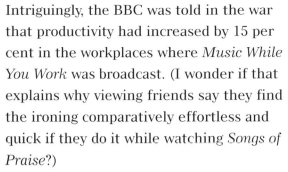

Intriguingly, the BBC was told in the war that productivity had increased by 15 per cent in the workplaces where *Music While You Work* was broadcast. (I wonder if that explains why viewing friends say they find the ironing comparatively effortless and quick if they do it while watching *Songs of Praise*?)

Different producers bring their own unique – sometimes quite eccentric – vision to the programmes, and there has been an enormous variety of approaches over the years. In the course of this book I shall be introducing you to many of these producers.

Simon Hammond, for example, produces *Songs of Praise* very much in the film-making style of Humphrey Jennings. His programmes contain many of the ingredients  that make *Songs of Praise* 'the nation's favourite' – by reflecting the colourful life in our churches that is still real,

but which for many is just a nostalgic memory. He is at his best making *Songs of Praise* in the British countryside, and for a few years he was responsible for an offshoot series called *Village Praise*, which looked at life and faith in rural areas. When Simon makes *Songs of Praise*, for every frost-rimmed sundial on-screen accompanied by the sound of birdsong and the voice of Laurie Lee reading from *Twelfth Night*, there will be footage of people dancing the hokey-cokey in Gloucester Cathedral. As well as a traditional pancake race, there is a portrait of a summer day when 15,000 Christians took over Cheltenham Racecourse. A vicar says that God is alive and well, not sleeping or dead, as he leads his congregation of eight in an ancient church in the Cotswolds. A few miles away another parish is praying for the families from their community that are working in Romania and Kosovo. Simon shows us a world full of messages, of conversations between old and new communities, and, as always, it is a world full of music.

For Hugh Faupel, after several years of editing *Songs of Praise*, diversity of programme style and location is the recipe for making a television series that claims to be the nation's favourite. Although he insists that every week's programme is first and last a musical celebration of faith, he also believes that surprise and new ways of looking at an old story are essential if an audience of all ages is to be attracted. In 1998,

BBC1 controller Peter Salmon expressed the network's aim as one where the audience 'must recognize themselves', and so threw out a challenge to producers to reflect the needs and enthusiasms of viewers from many cultures and faiths living in Britain in the third millennium.

New ways of looking at things, while at the same time allowing the audience to recognize themselves, are challenges that different *Songs of Praise* researchers, directors and producers over the years have relished. Programmes of new folk music appeared in the first 10 years. Then there were programmes, even in the early years, which, like the 2001 edition for Holocaust Sunday, brought together Christians and Jews. Also, there has always been music from Africa and from the Caribbean.

For example, in 1977 I was directing the film inserts for a *Songs of Praise* from Hackney, introduced by Michael Barratt. The researcher had reported that one depressed Catholic priest had said to her, 'The church of God is dead in Hackney.' The Methodists too were in a pretty parlous state at that time. The venue

**Songs of Praise Sings Gospel at Southwark Cathedral.**

*Left*: The final signal from floor manager Jeff Sluggett to conductor David Ogden as choirs in St Mary Redcliffe in Bristol burst into song.

*Above*: Jeff Sluggett explains the intricacies of the *Songs of Praise* rehearsal to the congregation.

had the whole place jumping. It was a new experience for the Anglican, Catholic and Methodist choirs in St John's – one I personally shall never forget – and must still be remembered by everyone who was there. I have never seen anything like it before – or since. The world has moved on and the contemporary, electronic 'anointed' music of Britain's black churches has replaced the strange beauty of that rollicking chorus produced by an amazing little choir

we were using for the hymns, the Church of St John-at-Hackney, was going through an interregnum and was in danger of closing. But we persevered and invited, as always, all the local churches of all denominations to send along their singers. Ray Short, the series producer, was directing the outside broadcast from St John's and I went along to help him. A choir from a small black Christian congregation in Hackney had been persuaded to come and join in the singing, because one of their members was being filmed choosing her hymn. Arriving rather nervously, they sat huddled together, but when they got going with performing their own song, culminating in a roaring chorus of 'O the Glory did roll', they

in Hackney, so obviously filled with the Holy Spirit.

Over the years, with programmes such as *Songs of Praise Sings Gospel* from Southwark Cathedral, and editions from places such as Detroit, Ghana, Zimbabwe and Jamaica, Christian choirs from different cultures have come with a growing confidence to help make the programme so richly varied.

'The hymn book is the place where the congregation strikes back,' said Colin Morris, former president of the Methodist Conference and for some years a distinguished head of religious broadcasting before becoming the BBC controller for Northern Ireland. He was preaching a sermon in Westminster Abbey at a service of thanksgiving celebrating 30 years of *Songs of Praise* in October 1991.

Taking words from Psalm 137, 'How shall we sing the Lord's song in a strange land?' he summed up *Songs of Praise* as a combination of two of the oldest forms of religion – common celebration and personal testimony – delivered by the latest technology. What was the secret, the 'it', that kept the programme popular in spite of growing competition from so many other channels? This is how Colin Morris described it in his sermon:

**Right**: Former series producer Helen Alexander finds one of the few parts of Australia where hymn-singing is not welcomed.

*Below*: Sydney Opera House, the setting for two special programmes marking the 2000 Olympics.

*The programme survives because people can often sing what they cannot say. That's why* Songs of Praise *counts its audience in more millions than there are regular churchgoers, because people can sing beyond their conscious beliefs. I remember a radical theologian in the 1960s being asked if he could say the Creed. 'No,' he replied, 'but I can sing it.' We can sing beyond our conscious beliefs because the many layers of meaning in music and poetry are able to accommodate all our agnosticism and doubt, our difficulty in swallowing precisely phrased theological propositions.*

*Confront the average chap with those sonorous phrases in the Creed, 'Very God of very God, begotten not made, being of one substance with the Father', and he'll say, 'Oh, all that's beyond me,' but give him 'Hark, the herald-angels sing' and he'll bellow with the best of them, 'Veiled in flesh the Godhead see, hail, th'incarnate Deity!'*

*So when millions of people who never darken the door of a church sit at home singing well-known and loved hymns on* Songs of Praise, *they are not being hypocritical or insincere. All kinds of strange, even contradictory, feelings and ideas – memories and hopes and longings – are gathered up in that potent combination of words and music. Words make things clear, but it's music that brings them alive. Words divide us into yea- and nay-sayers, believers and unbelievers, music unites us.*

So is *Songs of Praise* the nation's favourite? Ken Savidge, one of the first producers of *Songs of Praise* 40 years ago, remembers the eminent broadcaster and controller of the old BBC West Region, Frank Gillard, observing that he couldn't foresee many viewers wanting to watch *Sunday Half-Hour* (the long-running community hymn-singing programme) being photographed. After more than 1,700 editions, each watched by as many as six million viewers, and on a few occasions twice that number, with audiences still turning to BBC1 regularly on Sunday evenings, and a record choir of more than 60,000-strong singing in Cardiff's Millennium Stadium for the first edition broadcast in the year 2000, I think that surely *Songs of Praise* deserves its accolade.

Since a programme was made in New Zealand in the late 1960s, producers have travelled the world. With regular visits to Australia, where the programme is watched every Sunday morning on ABC Television, *Songs of Praise* has also been to Hong Kong and Shanghai, to South Africa, Zimbabwe and Ghana, as well as to Moscow, Berlin, Benidorm, the West Indies and the USA.

*Songs of Praise* has also regularly visited places the news journalists have described as trouble spots or places of social deprivation. Often it has been in these tough, inner-city communities that the most open-hearted

Producer Medwyn Hughes directing one of several *Songs of Praise* editions from Israel.

expressions of lively faith have been found.

I may not include a hymn in my *Desert Island Discs* choices, but I know what luxuries I would ask for. I shall be perfectly happy ever after with a solar-powered TV that only works on Sunday evening; I should be in heaven with a telephone that never rings on Sunday evening and, of course, an ironing board – but I don't think Sue Lawley allows *three* luxuries.

# In the Beginning...

## The Birth Pains of *Songs of Praise*

The first week of October 1961. Top of the pop-music charts were the Highwaymen, singing 'Michael', and on BBC TV there was a new series, *Songs of Praise*.

It was the beginning of the 'Swinging Sixties'. Twenty cigarettes cost four shillings and tuppence (less than 25 pence), a decent garden shed was on offer at 12 pounds and a complete garage with free construction was yours for 37 pounds. Colour television was being demonstrated for the first time at the National Radio Show in London's Earls Court. The *New English Bible* was a bestseller.

In the USA, Dr Martin Luther King, a Baptist preacher, was making world headlines in his campaign for equal rights for black and white people. His demonstrations of passive resistance – a 'campaign of love' – were waking people up, making everyone think.

Adam Faith was singing 'The Time Has Come', Nat 'King' Cole 'Let True Love Begin' and Helen Shapiro 'Walkin' Back to Happiness'. If you remember those songs, then you will remember that autumn of 1961.

It was a very frightening world at that time. In the late summer of 1961 Russian soldiers had formed a line separating East Berlin from the western part of the city. Within hours an ugly great concrete wall had gone up, dividing families and neighbours, with armed soldiers guarding it. Checkpoint Charlie became part of our language. Although the USA's President John F. Kennedy had met Russia's Premier Khrushchev at a summit conference in Vienna, the Cold War between the Soviet Bloc and the rest of the world was getting colder. In June, one of the world's greatest ever ballet dancers, Rudolph Nureyev, decided he preferred life in the West to that in Russia so made a dramatic bid for freedom in Paris. It would have seemed fantastic and unbelievable then if we had been told that a new BBC television programme to be launched that autumn would be broadcast from a non-Communist Moscow 30 years later.

The BBC was celebrating two 21st birthdays that year. First, *Radio Newsreel*, which had begun in the darkest days of the

Second World War, and secondly another radio programme, which had never been given a very glamorous billing in the *Radio Times*, *Sunday Half-Hour*. This weekly broadcast of community hymn-singing had begun with the hymn, 'We love the place, O God', sung in the church of St Mary Redcliffe, Bristol, on a stormy night just hours before the city was terribly bombed. *Radio Newsreel* is long gone, but *Sunday Half-Hour* survived to celebrate its 60th anniversary; and in 2001 *Songs of Praise*,

For 40 years choirs have been told never to look at the cameras, which was a tall order at this 1969 recording in St John's Church, Renfield, in Glasgow.

its junior partner, came from St Mary Redcliffe in a rebuilt Bristol.

Songs of Praise was launched at 6.15 p.m. on the first Sunday of October 1961. It came from the Tabernacle Baptist Church in Cardiff. Congregational hymn-singing was conducted by Mansel Thomas, solos were sung by the soprano Heather Harper and the programme was introduced by the Reverend Dr Gwilym ap Robert, who was already very popular with Welsh viewers and listeners.

That week's *Radio Times* promoted the beginning of BBC television's autumn schedule, marking the time when the nights begin to draw in and viewers were more likely to be indoors. 'This week, new shows begin and old favourites return to fall into the programmes like autumn leaves,' wrote the editor. The BBC was very conscious of competition from the new ITV companies. Just one day before the first *Songs of Praise* went out on air, a new station, Grampian Television, opened offering a choice of viewing for the first time to thousands of viewers in the north and east of Scotland. Grampian's competition with the very first *Songs of Praise* was not intense, with viewers simply being offered an edited version of a church service held in the new Aberdeen studio to dedicate its facilities. Today *Songs of Praise* still thrives, even though it now has to compete for viewers with four terrestrial channels and an increasing number of satellite ones.

**How it all began**

So where did *Songs of Praise* come from? Legend has it that it came about by accident when, in the summer of 1961, Donald Baverstock, the newly appointed assistant to the controller of BBC Television (Stuart Hood), was distracted and transfixed for a few moments during a visit to London's Crystal Palace transmitter by a recording of hymn-singing in Welsh. 'What is this?' he demanded, himself a Welshman but apparently unaware or forgetting that the Crystal Palace transmitter at that time showed a handful of TV programmes in Welsh for the benefit of the London-Welsh population. One

Welsh viewer writing to the *Radio Times* that summer, however, certainly knew about it. Describing himself as 'an exile in Sussex', he wrote to express admiration for what was a Sunday lunchtime TV series of hymn-singing in Welsh, describing it as 'the greatest programme in the entire range of BBC broadcasting'. He enthused about 'seeing the light of heaven in the eyes and in the demeanour of ordinary men, women and children'.

Now it is unlikely that the BBC, although ever-sensitive in responding to its viewers, tabled this letter at a top management meeting. But Donald Baverstock had an instinct for popular programme-making, and something about that brief glimpse of the Welsh hymn-singing had given him an idea. As a current affairs producer, he had in the mid-1950s devised *Tonight*, the weekday, early-evening TV programme where hard news was mixed with gentle and often humorous reports from around the world, all presided over by the genial Cliff Michelmore (later also to become a *Songs of Praise* presenter). Baverstock's *Tonight* cleverly caught the spirit of Britain and its nations, starring reporters such as Trevor Philpott, Alan Whicker and Scotland's Fyfe Robertson.

The convictions of another of the BBC's current affairs team suggest that *Songs of Praise* was an idea whose time had come. The late John Morgan, a formidable *Panorama* reporter of the 1960s, was a gently spoken

Celt who liked rugby, Wales and singing Nonconformist hymns, although he always added that he had not been inside a church for 20 years. Nevertheless, he became an early advocate for a programme of community hymn-singing.

There was another problem for the BBC television service that a programme of hymn-singing from churches and chapels around the nations of Britain might solve. Large outside-broadcast units were essential for the increasing coverage of Saturday sport and weekday racing, which took them and their crews all over Britain, but how could they be used on Sundays? Stuart Hood and Donald Baverstock thought they had the answer, and the next move was to try what BBC memos of the time describe as 'a choral music series involving the regions' and also as '*Sing His Praises*'. One weekday afternoon in the newly opened BBC Television Centre in Shepherd's Bush, a meeting agreed it was to be '*Songs of Praise*'. There would be no problems. Everyone was happy.

Strangely, it was the religious broadcasting department – destined to make the programmes – that was not happy. Their flagship programme was *Meeting Point*, which took a serious and considered view of religion in the world. It was a series for penetrating debate and awkward questions, mixed now and then with some

**A CLEAN KILL**

A research chemist devises a new detergent
that he decides to sell for a high price.
His wife tries to stop the deal but is
poisoned—who murdered her?

**TONIGHT'S PLAY
AT 8.15**

## OCTOBER 1 SUNDAY
## BBC tv evening

**BEGINNING TONIGHT**

**WHAT'S MY LINE?**
*
at 9.30

**6.5**
**SUNDAY STORY**
The Story of David
told by Cyril Fletcher
1: The Youngest Son
Script by CHAD VARAH
Produced by
JOHN ELPHINSTONE-FYFFE
BBC recording

**6.10**
**THE NEWS**

**6.15**
**SONGS OF PRAISE**
Congregational hymn-singing
from
TABERNACLE BAPTIST CHAPEL,
CARDIFF
with
Heather Harper (soprano)
Conducted by Mansel Thomas
Organist, V. Anthony Lewis
Introduced by
the Rev. Dr. Gwilym ap Robert
Produced by
GETHYN STOODLEY THOMAS
BBC recording
See page 12

**6.55**
**MEETING POINT**
Coping with Life
The Rev. Dr. Hugh Douglas
talks about pools, planets, pills
—and Providence
Produced by
the Rev. Dr. RONALD FALCONER
BBC recording
From Scotland

**Cyril Fletcher**
Tells the story
of David
in
'Sunday Story'
this evening
at 6.5

**7.25**
**THE NEWS**

**7.30**
**THE KAY STARR
ENGLISH MUSIC-HALL**
featuring America's dynamic
singing personality
**KAY STARR**
with
**DERYCK GUYLER
JACK BILLINGS AND
GEORGE BARON
THE GALLOW GLASS
CEILI BAND**
The Beryl Stott Singers
The Irving Davies Dancers
and
Woolf Phillips and his Orchestra
Dance director, Irving Davies
Script by BRAD ASHTON
Sets designed by Lionel Radford
Associate producer, Hal Stanley
Produced by RICHARD AFTON
BBC recording
See page 12

**8.15**
**THE
SUNDAY-NIGHT PLAY**
presents
**EMRYS JONES
PETRA DAVIES
BARRY LETTS
EDWARD WOODWARD**
in
**A Clean Kill**
by MICHAEL GILBERT
with
**Helen Christie
Laurence Hardy
Carmel McSharry**
Produced by David J. Thomas
*Cast in order of appearance:*
Ann Patten.................PETRA DAVIES
Charles Reese..............EMRYS JONES
Hilda Reese............HELEN CHRISTIE
Mrs. Turvey........CARMEL McSHARRY
Mr. Schofield.............BARRY LETTS
Mr. Senior.............LAURENCE HARDY
Superintendent Morland
                    EDWARD WOODWARD
Police Constable..EIFION WYN JONES
Film cameraman, Russell Walker
Film editor, Douglas Mair
Designer, David Butcher
From Wales
BBC recording
The quarrel Hilda Reese had with her
husband over the sale of his newly
patented cleaning fluid had unexpected
and even fatal results, but things took
an even more serious turn when
Superintendent Morland was called in
to investigate.
See page 13

**9.30**
**WHAT'S MY LINE?**
Chairman,
Eamonn Andrews
*Panel:*
**Isobel Barnett
Barbara Kelly
David Nixon**
A Guest Panellist
and
a mystery guest celebrity
Research by Julia Cave
Directed by Sydney Lotterby
Produced by JOHN WARRINGTON
Devised by
Mark Goodson and Bill Todman
Televised by arrangement with CBS
and Maurice Winnick
See page 13

**9.55**
**THE NEWS**

**10.5**
**JULIETTE GRECO**
sings of
Love and Lost Love
on the Left Bank of Paris
accompanied by
Henri Patterson
and his Ensemble
The Club St. Germain sequence
staged by Eleanor Fazan
Designer, Stanley Dorfman
Producer, James Gilbert
BBC recording
See page 12

**10.35**
**THE LABOUR PARTY
CONFERENCE**
Kenneth Harris and Robert Kee
discuss the Conference
that starts tomorrow
From the Headquarters Hotel
of the Labour Party in Blackpool
Associate producer, Jack Ashley
Produced by JOHN GRIST
See page 12

**10.45**
**THE EPILOGUE**
Prayers for the family
Conducted by
the Rev. William M. Macartney,
Minister of
St. Machar's Cathedral,
Old Aberdeen
BBC recording
From Scotland
SANDALE, PONTOP PIKE, DIVIS:
10.45-10.50 *The Epilogue: Problems
of Prayer. A talk by the Chaplain-
in-Chief, Royal Air Force*
10.50 *The Weather Man; Close Down*

**10.53**
**THE WEATHER
AND CLOSE DOWN**

★
**AT 7.30**
An American
singer tries
her hand at
English
Music-Hall
**KAY STARR**
★

★
**AT 10.5**
The Parisienne
cabaret star
from the
Left Bank
**JULIETTE
GRECO**

fine documentary programmes on film. They didn't think a series of weekly jolly hymn-sings was taking religion sufficiently seriously, although once or twice there had been an unwitting glimpse of the future, when *Meeting Point* from the Welsh TV studio had been devoted to choirs singing hymn requests and achieved a very big audience.

The record of correspondence between the top-floor management and the head of religious broadcasting at the time, the late Canon Roy McKay, reveals that quite a battle was fought over the establishment of *Songs of Praise* as the new complement to *Meeting Point* in the Sunday-evening TV schedule. This early-evening period was still 'closed' to all except religious output. Canon McKay felt that his territory was being invaded and told Stuart Hood that he would resign from the BBC in the most public way possible unless he was brought fully into the debate about the replacement of his own series, *Sunday Special*, with Donald Baverstock's hymn-singing innovation. His anger is perhaps understandable since he led a skilled team

who shared his view that the spirit of the 1960s meant challenge before comfort. Donald and Stuart dug their heels in. Ken Savidge, one of the first *Songs of Praise* producers, remembers hearing that they had said, 'OK. If you don't want to do it, we'll give it to Light Entertainment.' It was a threat too far. Planning began under the slightly distant supervision of Canon McKay, working mostly with his regional producers.

The religious broadcasting department producers had a point. They wanted to make serious, consciousness-raising programmes. The controllers, then and now, always want 'popular' programmes. The faith communities all want – and demand – that their own views be represented. Only a few years after the birth of *Songs of Praise* the then archbishop of York, the late Dr Donald Coggan, publicly described TV religious producers as '*ignorami* broadcasting for the benefit of the gormless masses'. Forty years on, BBC controllers still make their own unilateral decisions, which fortunately continue to favour *Songs of Praise*. Voices in the UK's faith communities are still

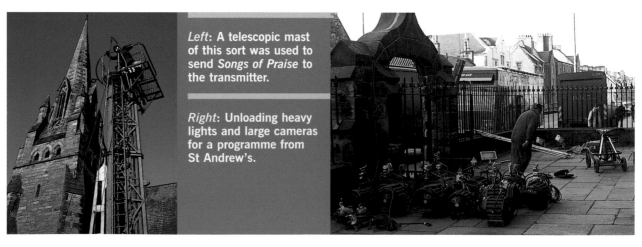

**Left**: A telescopic mast of this sort was used to send *Songs of Praise* to the transmitter.

**Right**: Unloading heavy lights and large cameras for a programme from St Andrew's.

raised now and again in fury at the coverage of religion, both at what is made and at what is missing. But *Songs of Praise* took off like a rocket, with an immediate audience numbering millions. By the end of its first decade, as many as 20 million viewers had meant it had broken all records for audiences for religious broadcasting.

One person who was particularly keen on *Songs of Praise* from the first and who was to produce literally hundreds of programmes both for Scotland as well as for the BBC network was Ronald Falconer. Dr Falconer, or 'Ronnie' as he was known throughout the Scottish churches in his 25 years of leading BBC Scotland's religious broadcasting team, had been a Church of Scotland minister in Coatdyke, in the heart of coal-mining and steel-making Lanarkshire. To Ronnie Falconer, *Songs of Praise* was an absolutely ideal programme to show Presbyterianism at its very best, with its great tradition of congregational praise. After all, great moments in the history of the Scottish nation had been marked with the singing of hymns, paraphrases and psalms. There was the metrical version of Psalm 124, 'Now Israel may say, and that truly', sung by the Reformers in 16th-century Edinburgh at the time of John Knox. There were also verses from Psalm 43, 'O send forth thy light and thy truth', to the tune 'Martyrs', sung at the Disruption in 1843 (when ministers had stood up for biblical principles and marched out of the church's General Assembly).

These words and simple tunes, sung by ordinary, God-fearing people, would convey the soul of Scotland to the rest of the world. Ronnie was no wistful sentimentalist either, for he was making programmes at a time when church membership, especially in Scotland, was actually growing. While the London religious broadcasting team had their misgivings, Ronnie Falconer, when on a visit to Glasgow in the summer of 1961, lobbied Stuart Hood to go ahead with his new series.

One of the first editions of *Songs of Praise*

The Reverend Dr Ronald Falconer (second from left) directing and vision-mixing with his top BBC Scotland team.

from Scotland came from the shipbuilding town of Greenock, with the voices, as the *Radio Times* billing went, of 'the men young and old of the Cartsburn-Augustine and East Congregational Churches'. It was a little misleading as there were women present too, but sadly the original tape, like all *Songs of Praise* programmes of the first few years, has not survived; and all this being long before the days of home videos means there is no record apart from viewers' memories.

Ralph Smith, another Church of Scotland minister, was recruited by Ronnie Falconer to direct an ever-increasing number of broadcasts in Scotland. He remembers the way he used to make *Songs of Praise*. Ideally, four large cameras would be mounted in fixed positions side by side, or on scaffolding one above the other, facing the congregation. Ronnie loved directing the cameras, vision-mixing himself and cutting on the beat from one camera to another. One or two hymns, he insisted, must always be 'off the cuff', picking out the best close-ups the camera crew had to offer. These inevitably included the young women the cameramen had most taken a fancy to. Ronnie would often have to say on the talk-back, 'No, Camera 3, we must not see that blonde again!'

'I learned the craft of mixing and writing a camera script by watching Ronnie,' says Ralph. He showed me a primitive director's lens he had invented – a piece of cardboard with a TV-shaped hole cut out of it, attached to a length of knotted string – which he always used to plan his shots. 'For the widest shot, I placed my eye by the first knot and looked through the cardboard aperture.' Ralph usually tried to complete this process out of sight of curious, even suspicious, church officers or mocking cameramen.

There was another first for *Songs of Praise* that Ronnie pioneered. He had a Leica camera and loved taking photographs of his beloved Scotland in all its moods. The stills

January 2001: Ralph Smith is reunited with his 1969 DIY shot-planner.

mounted on caption boards would be shown during the opening hymn, mixing from one beautiful vista to another, setting the scene. Later, when colour TV was introduced, he used slide-projectors, operated from inside the church.

But Scotland wanted to offer even more of its beautiful landscape to network viewers. How about a *Songs of Praise* from the remote Hebriddean island of Iona, where St Columba had landed to bring Christianity to Scotland? The challenge was formidable. How could the BBC Scotland outside-broadcast unit – two or three huge pantechnicons full of camera, sound and lighting equipment – get onto the island? The only ferry was far too small.

First, Ronnie and his technical managers set about trying to hire a 'puffer', the small steam coasters used locally. But a puffer had a deep hold and its derrick could not cope with lifting a massive truck. It seemed impossible. Then someone remembered that St Columba had first come to Iona by coracle, landing on a beach in Martyrs' Bay. The nearest equivalent was a tank-landing craft – and this is how such a war-like vessel came to be used by *Songs of Praise* for the peaceful purpose of marking the 1,400th anniversary of the arrival on land of a Celtic saint. When *Songs of Praise* was successfully transmitted from Iona in May 1963, Ronnie and the whole BBC Scotland crew were triumphant. Many times since then *Songs of Praise* has been back to Iona, and now it is as easy as driving up the motorway, but no one who took part will forget the first epic voyage on a tank-landing craft in the steps of St Columba.

While there were pioneers from the church, like Ronnie Falconer and Ray Short, most *Songs of Praise* programmes in the first years were made by producers who directed outside broadcasts of every description. They might be directing the Grand National one day and *Songs of Praise* the next, or come straight from directing a Christmas circus, or producing *Come Dancing* or Crufts Dog Show. Most of the earliest editions of *Songs of Praise* came from what the BBC used to call 'the regions'. Michael Meech, then a TV newsreader in Bristol and now a popular broadcaster currently on BBC local radio, remembers introducing one of the first programmes from the Portsmouth Guildhall. Between his shots on camera to introduce the hymns, he dabbed himself from a bottle of eau-de-cologne, since it was very hot under the lights. Immediately an outraged hall-keeper rushed over protesting, 'There's no alcohol allowed in here!' Not long afterwards, on the coldest and snowiest of January nights in Worthing, *Songs of Praise* for Easter Sunday was being recorded. Michael remembers that on such a freezing night it was a challenge to convey the flavour of spring and Christ's resurrection.

*Songs of Praise* was clearly proving an

The first BBC Scotland outside-broadcast unit on Iona. The size and number of vehicles explain the need for a tank-landing craft to get to the island.

enjoyable experience for viewers in every part of Britain. Meeting in March 1962, for the first time after the series began the previous October, the Central Religious Advisory Committee, made up of representatives from different church denominations, rather coolly agreed that 'naturalness and a touch of informality' were 'allies of *Songs of Praise*', increasing its appeal for 'non-churchgoers and fringe Christians'.

The same august body, however, meeting again not long after that, took a sideswipe at

Ray Short with the TV directors' new plaything of the 1960s, the zoom lens.

another popular broadcast, Sandy McPherson's weekly radio programme *The Chapel in the Valley*, whose 'religiosity', they thought, 'did a disservice to the religion that many depend on for comfort'. This programme, which was not produced by religious broadcasters, for years captivated a huge audience who found comfort in Sandy's evocation of a friendly Brigadoon-like chapel, peopled by implausibly devout people with the most golden of voices. Unlike

the newly launched *Songs of Praise* it was indeed a myth, constructed not in the Welsh valleys but in the Jubilee Chapel, Hoxton, in London's East End, which, after surviving wartime bombing, became the home of the BBC Theatre Organ. Sandy McPherson, who had broadcast almost without ceasing in the first uneasy days of the Second World War, had become part of the fabric of the BBC's radio programmes with his *Twilight Hour*.

A letter to the *Radio Times* early in 1940 summed up the appetite for programmes that even today still seem to have a place. 'May we have a programme of sacred music, say half an hour of the old hymn tunes? I find we never get them unless we switch over to Hilversum [a Dutch station]. Why go abroad when we have as magnificent an organist as Sandy McPherson?'

Years later some *Songs of Praise* viewers still ask for programmes to fit the same bill. So programmes devoted to the life and music of people like Moody and Sankey have been recorded in a make-believe setting with everyone in Victorian costumes. Religious programme-makers today looking to the different needs of their audiences know only too well the hazardous and wobbly course they must steer between programmes that bring comfort and programmes that disturb and awaken dull minds.

Ray Short, who in 1970 became the first series producer (now called editor) of *Songs of Praise*, describes his taste in music as 'low', and although he has a good tenor voice and grew up singing solos in chapels, remembers programmes being criticized because the singing was far too good. 'Don't let *Songs of Praise* sound like a choral society,' he would say to the team. 'It should sound like the way congregations would like to think they do sound – but, in fact, don't!' Ray's first outside broadcast did not go too smoothly. It was a live broadcast from Lancaster and things kept going wrong: 'I felt as if I was chasing the programme, which was gradually escaping from me.' An elderly parson was to do the blessing, but in rehearsal he kept missing the place where he was to stand so that a camera could see him. Ray thought he had the solution: 'I put a penny on the floor and told him to walk forward and stand on it to speak his words. Came the moment, and there he was, creeping forward very, very slowly towards my camera, bent down almost double to try to find my wretched penny! It looked very odd, but I learned that I had a lot to learn.'

To this day, that is the 11th commandment for all *Songs of Praise* producers: you have a lot to learn.

I remember being astonished, when I first became editor, by a letter from a viewer who deplored any introduction of new music, and also added his plea to a by-then growing and vigorous lobby that we superimpose the words of hymns on the screen. Every Sunday in his south-coast town, he assured me, he and around 999 other home-organ enthusiasts were at their keyboards accompanying *Songs of Praise*. I have searched in vain for evidence of the other 999, but perhaps before long, in the new on-line age, an enterprising *Songs of Praise* producer will link up all these musicians.

**Each verse or line of every hymn is allocated a camera shot, the result of hours of planning.**

---

Camera: 2

| Prog No: | 01/NMG F442D | Title: | SONGS OF PRAISE |
| Date: | 11th February 2001 | Subtitle: | |

| SHOT | POS | DESCRIPTION | NOTES |

SEQ 1. CHRIST IS MADE THE SURE FOUNDATION
TUNE: 'WESTMINSTER ABBEY'
FIRST PASS

| SHOT | POS | DESCRIPTION |
|---|---|---|
| | | CAM.2 IN POS.A |
| 2 | A | L/A tight 2-shot trumpets & gentle dev. to include musos (4 bars) |
| | | MOVE TO POS.B DURING SHOT 3 |
| 7 | B | L/A 10-shot + pillar cong. J/M |
| 10 | B | L/A 2-shot cong.M |
| 13 | B | MWS looking NW fav. cong. J/M + pillars |
| 16 | B | MCU single Cong. M |

Page 1

# The Birds Take Over

## The Secret World of *Songs of Praise* Technicians

'I want a tern in the north transept, a kestrel in the middle of the nave… and do you think we could wedge an osprey into the space between the statue of Our Lady and the high altar?'

Every few weeks, somewhere in the world – usually in a church – a new edition of *Songs of Praise* is being planned from scratch. All professions have their own specialist language, none perhaps more exotic than that used by television technicians. Gone are the days of fixed lenses on largely stationary cameras mounted on scaffolding. Today's cameras swoop and glide. So welcome to the bird world of BBC outside broadcasts.

**Strange encounters**

Churches always seem to be at their darkest and coldest for the initial planning meeting, and the little party standing in the middle of the building on a winter weekday keep their anoraks on. I remember many days when our breath emerged like steam in the still, quiet, but absolutely arctic interior of an ancient

church. Clergy or churchwardens, who had come along to see what they were letting themselves in for now that their *Songs of Praise* invitation had been taken up, would hover nervously on the edge of the party.

So how were these birds going to be used? Why were we peering up at the roof, sometimes even with binoculars, and pacing the gap between the pews, arguing hotly over whether it measured three feet nine inches or three feet nine and a half inches? Now, we might be scrutinizing the Victorian iron gratings over the heating system. 'Good Lord!' gasps an alarmed parson. 'Does that man really need to jump up and down on them?'

Over the years when I was directing *Songs of Praise*, I always tried to dissuade the clergy and churchwardens from coming along to those weird planning meetings. It is the beginning of a quite baffling conversation – for them – between the camera director and the BBC's technical operations manager. This is the moment in which the imagination of the director comes up against all the technical difficulties and practical challenges of getting cameras and lights into a church designed in another age. It's the director's job to introduce the 15th-century architect to the 21st-century engineer. By the time of the recording, they must be working in total harmony. As the planning meeting gets to grips with working out how to fit up to six cameras in, the BBC team tries to explain its trade secrets to our hosts. Birds will not be flying around the choirboys, but cameras mounted on superbly engineered mobile equipment will. So a TV camera fitted on a tern or a teal will glide past the soloist and then 'duck' down out of sight of the kestrel, which carries another camera, hovering at a great height looking at the hundreds of singers below before dropping down to peer sideways along a single row. The dolphin will leap from the close-up of the harpist's hands to the elegant fingering of a French horn. All these 'birds' are pedestals and trolleys fitted with complex hydraulics especially designed to carry TV cameras. Sensitive camera moves timed to the split second are only made possible by some of the world's most gifted and experienced television crews. Every *Songs of Praise* depends on them.

In the third millennium, *Songs of Praise* makes use of the latest state-of-the-art techniques. Long, carefully counterbalanced lightweight arms swing small cameras up to the rafters, relying on teamwork between one person controlling the gentle move and another who will be remotely manipulating the camera to zoom in to a window detail out of sight except through a small TV monitor. It is art and science brought together in moments of intense concentration, and the camera crew, who will spend the programme dodging around choirs and congregations, know that any mistake on their part that leads to a retake could be the final straw for hard-working

Former editor Roger Hutchings with Peter Webb the lighting director and Graham Haines the sound supervisor.

singers giving their all. Camera operators are particularly unforgiving of their own mistakes. Even the best is only just good enough for *Songs of Praise*.

Sometimes the most beautiful shot is unplanned, emerging when a camera operator notices something that no one else has seen. The newest cranes and cameras, which can operate at low light level, are particularly effective in ancient churches where the quality of the medieval architects' skill and imagination may be seen for the first time since the builders finished work centuries ago. On one occasion a camera focused on a beautiful stuffed owl placed high up in a dark roof centuries ago to discourage bats. Nobody had seen it before. Sometimes there will be the first glimpse under the light of a long-concealed medieval wall-painting.

Lighting for *Songs of Praise* is now a highly developed art and a small band of experienced lighting directors bring the skill of the artist to contrasting the light and the shade in every church. More than that, they try to make everyone look good, whether in the widest shot or in a big close-up. Whether you like hymn-singing or not, catch only the final minutes of an episode of *Songs of Praise* as the credits roll and if the names Bernie Davis, Pete Webb, Geoff Stafford or Jim McNamee are listed, then you will have missed seeing some beautiful television.

Positioning the camera in St Mary Redcliffe for John Kirby's 'miracle shot'.

Take a recent programme from Bristol. While the choirs are rehearsing, Geoff Stafford is trying to work out how John Kirby, the director, can crane a remotely operated camera from ground level behind the high altar, first to show a stand laden with prayer candles, then on up past the huge altar cross and then even higher, to reveal the whole of the congregation gathered in St Mary Redcliffe. This is one of Britain's most beautiful churches, according to Queen Elizabeth I. The camerawork sounds hard enough, but the real problem is how Geoff is going to light this previously unplanned shot. Geoff, who recently lit the Sydney Opera House effortlessly, is being put on the spot.

Sitting in the dark in the south transept, peering at a console crammed with twinkling red and green lights showing which of the lamps high up in the roof are already in use, he is consulting a huge chart and shaking his head gravely. With the smallest note of irritation in his voice, he's whispering into a microphone that links him with John Kirby in the control van. How, he asks, can he be expected to light the altar for the shot without the camera seeing the carefully positioned lights which are to bring out its ornate features? If the lights are on, the camera will see the cross and the altar but not the church, and if they are off, the altar will be invisible. 'Make your choice,' he says. 'It can't be done.'

And then he adds, before John can speak to make his unenviable choice, 'OK, we'll see what we can do.'

He turns to Martin Rourke, his lighting colleague. 'You had better start practising now to get those lights on and off in the split second between the shots.' In the final programme, seen a week or so later, the impossible shot is there for all to enjoy. So beautiful, in fact, that the director used it several times. On *Songs of Praise* with Geoff, Bernie, Pete and Jim, you don't even wait for the impossible. So behind those pictures and the all-important but invisible sound-recording lie impressive teamwork and a great deal of elbow grease.

When the time comes to start work in earnest, it is the lighting director's team that arrives first to disturb the ecclesiastical peace. Specialist scaffolders hang bars in seemingly inaccessible places for as many as several hundred lights, which must be positioned so that viewers never see them, even though shots are taken from many different angles. This is a somewhat tall order in some churches, although the taller the building, the easier it can be to hide lamps. (The lighting director's team must also have a head for heights.) They face at least two days' hard labour carrying lamps up long ladders, and to light a cathedral can be a week's work. It is a noisy and often messy process as each lamp is switched on and positioned precisely so that it will bring out the best features of every singer. As it is so hazardous, faithful parishioners intent on arranging flowers and polishing brass need to be discouraged, although many come to watch in fascination.

The outside-broadcast technicians whose names never appear on-screen often come as close as any of the production team to the local community in the unglamorous hours before a *Songs of Praise* recording. I'm thinking of the night before Mothering Sunday in March 1997,

when Dunblane Cathedral was a place for grieving. Immediately after the dreadful attack on the children of the town's primary school that week, bewildered and tearful people came to sit in the nave. Everyone wanted to help, but few knew what to do. The local Salvation Army, as ever recognizing practical needs, placed little packs of tissues on each pew. The cathedral was the centre not just for a town, but for a nation in shock.

*Songs of Praise* was to be broadcast the next day, in a special edition. I watched as the outside-broadcast crew for BBC Scotland completed a week's work in a day. By contrast to the normal cheery bustle, they worked gently and in complete silence. Pointing and gesturing to each other at the top of their spindly ladders, they occupied only one pew at a time as they lit the cathedral nave.

Then I realized that they were doing something else too. People in ones and twos were glancing up and coming over to the team. They needed someone who had the time to listen and who, unlike the rest of the world's media milling around outside the cathedral, would not ask questions. They found a sympathetic ear from technicians who were already facing the challenge of their lives. Next day, it was those same technicians who rushed the same lamps out of the cathedral at record-breaking speed to ensure that the Queen's meeting with the

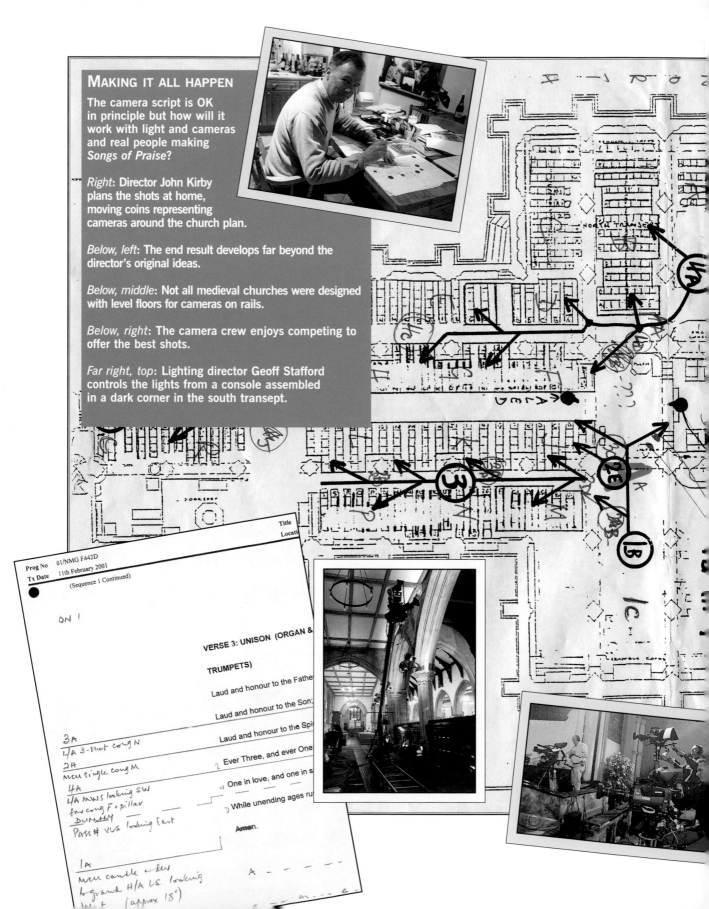

## MAKING IT ALL HAPPEN

The camera script is OK in principle but how will it work with light and cameras and real people making *Songs of Praise*?

*Right*: Director John Kirby plans the shots at home, moving coins representing cameras around the church plan.

*Below, left*: The end result develops far beyond the director's original ideas.

*Below, middle*: Not all medieval churches were designed with level floors for cameras on rails.

*Below, right*: The camera crew enjoys competing to offer the best shots.

*Far right, top*: Lighting director Geoff Stafford controls the lights from a console assembled in a dark corner in the south transept.

Prog No   01/NMG F442D
Tx Date   11th February 2001
(Sequence 1 Continued)

ON 1

VERSE 3: UNISON (ORGAN & TRUMPETS)

Laud and honour to the Fathe

Laud and honour to the Son;

Laud and honour to the Spir

Ever Three, and ever One

One in love, and one in s

While unending ages ru

Amen.

3A
L/A 3-shot cong N

2A
MCU single cong M

4A
L/A MWS looking SW
fav cong F + pillar
DUMMY
PASS # VLS looking East

1A
MCU candle + lev
to grand H/A LS looking
West (approx 18°)

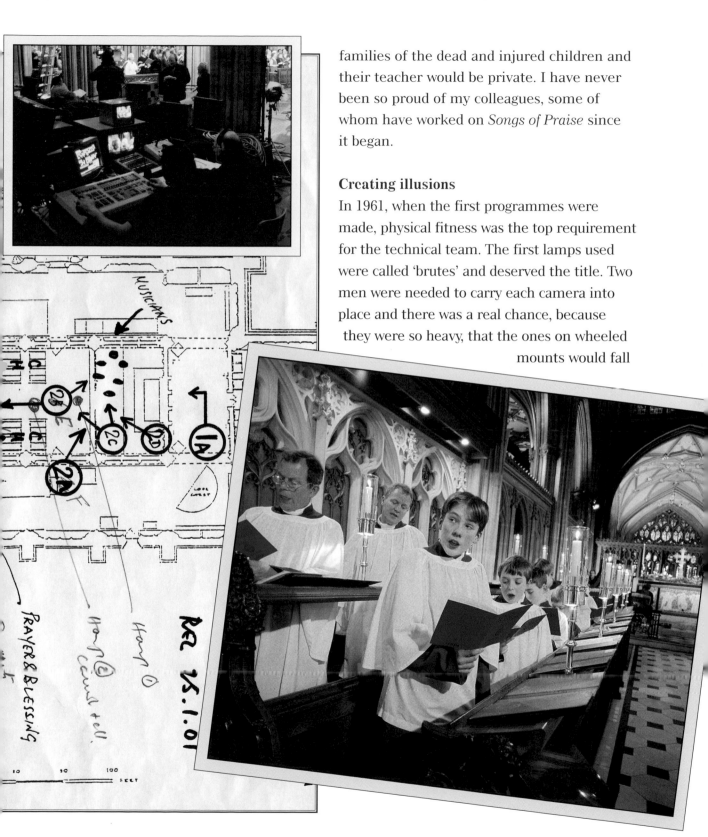

families of the dead and injured children and their teacher would be private. I have never been so proud of my colleagues, some of whom have worked on *Songs of Praise* since it began.

### Creating illusions

In 1961, when the first programmes were made, physical fitness was the top requirement for the technical team. The first lamps used were called 'brutes' and deserved the title. Two men were needed to carry each camera into place and there was a real chance, because they were so heavy, that the ones on wheeled mounts would fall through the Victorian ironwork onto fragile but essential heating pipes.

Every week, directors and cameramen fought to keep their cameras out of each other's shots, but the equipment was so huge and needed to be so close to the action to get the right shots that something would always go wrong. Worse, instead of a single zoom lens of the sort everyone now has on their camcorder, these black-and-white monster cameras had a range of 'fixed' lenses and the camera operator had to manipulate a lever to select everything from a wide angle to a close-up.

It was the cause of much grief if the director was in any way unclear in asking for the shot that was needed. Some older, unkind colleagues of mine remember that they could guess who was directing by counting the number of shots that were taken with a camera in mid-lens-change. In those days there were no funds to edit the 'gaffs' out of *Songs of Praise*, and what the viewer saw during the lens-change is best described as similar to the

moment at the optometrist's when different lenses are swiftly flicked in front of the patient's eyes. I still remember the work of one director, who always inadvertently provided viewers with images of all the camera crew as they sailed gracefully through each other's shots at a stately pace to match the hymn-singing. Never losing his nerve (or perhaps never noticing?), the shot would sometimes be held until the dalek-like 20th-century invader vanished behind a medieval pillar.

Nowadays, camera lenses and clever operators perform what seem like miracles. Space-age technology also helps *Songs of Praise*. It allowed a camera on a hill high above Dartmouth, looking at a view of most of south Devon, to zoom in to show half-a-dozen singers several miles away at a waterfront recording. The shot nearly came to grief because of the behaviour of some cows that came so close to the cameraman they blocked the shot, presumably resenting the intrusive presence of the BBC in their field.

Other kinds of 'miracles' have also been seen by viewers of *Songs of Praise*. They have telephoned and written to us about seeing stained-glass windows in which the Blessed Virgin Mary has bowed her head in sorrow while on-screen; apostles and prophets, dormant since the artists completed their work, have raised a hand in blessing – or perhaps in condemnation, depending on the viewer's feelings.

In the end, I think *Songs of Praise* itself is a miracle of a sort. So much unseen mess to cope with, so much distraction for everyone taking part that must somehow be forgotten in the act of singing; the miracle of surprise that ensures no two programmes are ever exactly alike; and the miracle of the continuing goodwill of Christians all over the world prepared to come and join in – especially the blessed ones who come to strange preliminary technical meetings and welcome the tern, the dolphin and the kestrel.

*Above*: **Outside-broadcast camera with turret fixed lenses used in the first decade of *Songs of Praise*.**

*Left*: **Remotely operated lightweight camera on long 'jimmy-jib' arm achieves visual miracles in Alnwick Parish Church, 1998.**

# 'Don't Be the Yorkshire Pudding Choir!'

## *Songs of Praise* in the Making

**B**radford, on a cold, dark, weekday night in January 2001. Rehearsal for the first *Songs of Praise* recording of the new millennium is about to get underway in the West Riding city made famous by the composer Delius and the writer J.B. Priestley.

In his classic *English Journey*, Priestley travels back to Bradford, the city of his birth and childhood. On a wet Sunday night, he comes across a Salvation Army Band playing on a street corner and he reflects that if ever he could persuade himself to believe in the Christian account of life, 'I shall either join the Catholic Church or fall in with the Salvation Army.' *Songs of Praise* from Bradford would have gladdened Jack Priestley's heart, as the programme came from a Roman Catholic Church filled with Christian choirs from all the surrounding churches and accompanied by the stirring sound of a top Salvation Army Band.

**The stars are born**

'Now tonight, I want a bit more bounce,' is conductor Nigel Swinford's cheery opening demand of the huge choir arranged before him in St Mary's Church. Nigel is one of the BBC production team's most treasured assets, a musician who can, in little more than a couple of hours, encourage amateur singers and musicians who hardly know each other to perform on television as one large united sound.

This is a tense moment for everyone. It's the first night's full rehearsal. Since the brief rehearsal here last week for some of the choirs, the church has been transformed by television light with more than 100 lamps suspended from scaffold poles across the nave arches for a full TV rehearsal. 'I've been worshipping here since I was a child,' gasps someone as they come in, 'but I've never seen St Mary's look so beautiful.' And it does. In spite of the miles of cable and paraphernalia the outside-broadcast crew have brought with them, the church looks stunning. Wall-paintings, normally unnoticed under the church's own rather harsh but practical arc lights, stand out tonight as if freshly painted. Stone saints and angels have emerged overhead to look down benignly on the rows of singers in the pews and the television crew clustered around its four high-tech cameras.

So while other men and women around the city are settling down to watch the evening's soap operas, others here have come to join choirs from Bradford's many Christian churches. The Salvation Army Band of the West Hunslet Corps from nearby Leeds, the organist, the choir and the congregation, together with some mesmerizing and beautiful Indian dancers, all prepare to do what Nigel describes as rehearsing 'to within an inch of broadcast quality'. Almost there, but not quite, saving the very best of all that energy and talent for the actual recording the next night. Then they will aim to bring pleasure to millions of viewers all over Britain, and pride to the city. Only the best will do.

Just outside the city centre, St Mary's Roman Catholic Church stands at the head of Church Bank, a busy road dominated by Bradford's Anglican cathedral. Beyond the tired façade of the dental surgery, which comes straight from the world of Priestley's novel *Angel Pavement*, beyond the offices of the aptly located 'Congregational Insurance', just yards from the city centre, blocks of inner-city high-rise flats take over. East Parade is in a district where life can be hard. The technical vans from BBC Resources in Manchester are clustered up here around the Victorian bulk of St Mary's, right on top of what seems to be one of West Yorkshire's noisiest and busiest road junctions. At this same junction, while setting up over the previous day, the television crew has been enjoying hospitality in one of Bradford's good-news stories, the Cock and Bottle. It is one of Britain's very few Christian pubs, complete with its own upper room. It looks like the perfect 'olde worlde local', but supping beer while listening to the strains of the Christian charismatic chorus 'Majesty, worship his majesty' makes it a unique experience.

Across the road, as the rehearsal is about to begin, Father Michael, parish priest of St Mary's, calls the more than 700 excited singers to order. It has been an eventful few days for him too, with tons of broadcasting equipment being installed in his church and his usual calm routine completely disrupted. With as many as 800 parishioners at Mass every week, he has had to organize a raffle for congregation tickets to the programme, which takes place after Sunday Mass, and only about 1 in 10 of those who wanted to attend have been successful. 'Worse than the Last Night of the Proms,' someone observes.

'So let's calm down after such an exciting time, and take a deep, deep breath.' Suddenly there is calm as the priest, who has been quietly sitting in the congregation, unnoticed but for his dog collar, stands up and draws everyone, friend and stranger, together in prayer. 'We place ourselves, our hearts and our voices into your mind, Lord. May all we do reflect your glory so that we, together with all who watch in their homes, may know you as you really are.'

Minutes later, the heat is really turned up. Nigel, feeling a little frail after a recent illness, is nevertheless giving the 110 per cent familiar to the many Christian musicians who've worked with him over the years.

Off comes the jacket. 'This hymn', he says of 'I, the Lord of sea and sky', 'is God saying "hello".'

Off comes the pullover. 'This must be about smiling, and you don't look very happy at all. Don't be the Yorkshire pudding choir!'

Noticeably everything begins to improve, and with the resonance of the Salvation Army Band and the organ playing together, by the time we come to 'Sing of the Lord's goodness' everyone is having a go, even at the back. It is a long way to the back – almost 20 rows – and from there the conductor looks like a small, faraway windmill.

'Can you hear me?' shouts Nigel in a passable impersonation of Sandy Powell, the famous music-hall comedian, shouting, 'Can you hear me, Mother?'

'No, no, no!' A chorus from the back.

'Can't see you either,' comes another desperate cry from a distant part of St Mary's.

The conductor obligingly clambers up onto a higher box. 'But I can't be up here for the recording,' he bellows, fearing a spectacular TV collapse for a future edition of *Auntie's Bloomers*.

What matters is that *everyone* in the church takes part and can see and hear, because the cameras and microphones can see and hear everyone. There are no passengers on *Songs of Praise*.

Michael Wakelin, the new series producer of *Songs of Praise*, is in charge for the first time. He leaves the little hideaway where he has been anxiously watching every shot on a monitor, nervously fingering a walkie-talkie which keeps him in touch with David Taviner, the director. David is sitting in the scanner control van outside, talking the cameramen and senior sound and lighting engineers through each shot of the rehearsal.

Michael leaps up to the lectern during a break in the singing to reassure the most distant participants that they matter. 'Your face could tell the whole story of *Songs of Praise* from Bradford,' he tells them. 'And please don't even think of waving at the camera and Mum at home. We'll have to do the whole hymn again if you do.'

Michael has another worry. This Bradford *Songs of Praise* is meant to reflect the modern city of many cultures that is home to people from all over the world. Some will be featured in separately filmed interviews talking to the presenter, Diane-Louise Jordan. 'Where are they tonight?' Michael asks David, because none of these participants has turned up.

'Wait until the recording,' is the response from the director, who has the gift of sounding calm even when faced with problems from all directions. ('Not exactly how I feel,' David confides to me later.)

Tonight the director has some other little problems to solve. The conductor is asking everyone to clap as they sing what he calls the 'Clapping Gloria', a lively contemporary setting of ancient words. Robert Prizeman, the music advisor for *Songs of Praise*, who has been sitting quietly behind the audio supervisor who is balancing sound from stereo microphones concealed around the church, suddenly leaps to his feet. 'They are all out of time and they're too loud. We need a BBC clap.'

'What's that?' someone asks.

'Well,' says the director, who began his career in radio, 'it's a sort of delicate clap, which doesn't drown the voice. Though how you both clap and hold your hymn book is anybody's guess.'

Now that this is known to be everybody's problem, everyone has their own pet theory. Stan Royle, the floor manager, and the answer to all needs at any *Songs of Praise*

recording, has the winning solution to the dilemma: 'Hold your programme in one hand, and clap your neighbour's hand with the other.'

The choirs are quick to get the idea and the younger singers are soon having a ball. Near to Camera 2, two small girls turn away from the conductor for a spontaneous round of pat-a-cake. The cameraman obligingly offers a nicely framed shot of their very own BBC1 moment.

'Now,' says Nigel, who has long forgotten his recent ill-health, 'I just want you to sway a little bit more. Can we try it? You don't have to but...'

'And tell them,' says David, safe in his seat in the control van, 'if they don't clap, they won't be let out.'

'Shot 68 on Camera 2,' calls the director's assistant. 'Gosh, that woman on the end of the pew is really going for it.'

It is two hours since the rehearsal began and it's clear that Bradford's *Songs of Praise* is going to be a cracker.

## Apply within?

So can anyone join in and make *Songs of Praise* in their church? Twenty years ago, when I was the editor of the programme, there were always 100 or so outstanding invitations for the BBC to 'please consider televising a service of *Songs of Praise*'. Often the request was to coincide with the 'anniversary celebrations for our church'. Very often, particularly in the north of England, this was to mark a 100th anniversary, because so many churches there belong to the Victorian era.

Some writers were obviously regular viewers, but others recorded rather distantly that they had been 'instructed by the organizing committee to write and apply'. A flower festival might be being planned, and the suggestion was that *Songs of Praise* could be fitted in on the Sunday afternoon before clearing-up operations began. If the writer was a regular viewer, I suppose it was a compliment to everyone who had ever worked on *Songs of Praise* that it looked so effortless and spontaneous that it could be 'fitted in'. Would that making BBC1's flagship religious broadcast were so simple!

Some requests fell at the first hurdle. These were the honest invitations that concluded with something like, 'By the way – there's no parking allowed outside the

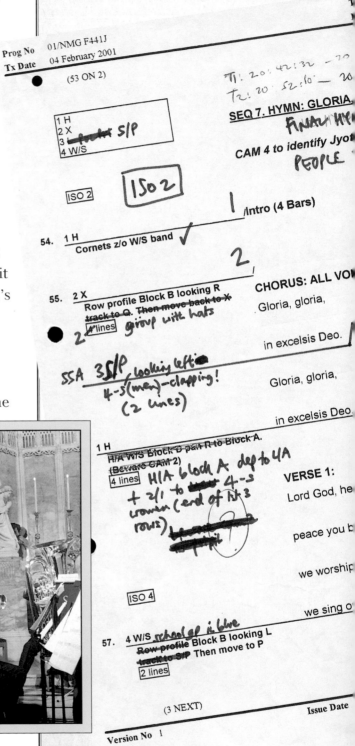

## PRAISE WITH MUSIC AND SONG

The producer wants everyone to sing, clap and hold their hymn books. Is he serious?

*Far left*: The front-line role for the West Hunslet Corps of the Salvation Army.

*Left*: Conductor Nigel Swinford gets to work on the 'Clapping Gloria'.

*Below, left*: Michael Wakelin wants everyone to be really happy in his first programme as series producer.

*Below, right*: Close teamwork between organist Paul Hanson and the conductor.

church, but a small car park within easy walking distance, reached by a footbridge across the river, could perhaps be coned off as our part-time verger is also a special constable.' Sadly, I had to disappoint such kindly, innocent correspondents. There were many really beautiful churches all over Britain from which we simply could not broadcast. In those days, with at least three huge vans to park – one of which had to be positioned within yards of the church door and from which massive cables linked up with the TV cameras inside – the BBC's arrival to record *Songs of Praise* would have

British troops give out hymn-sheets and sing along with Christian Aid workers in *Songs of Praise* from Cizre in Turkey, near the border with Iraq, in spring 1991.

provided many a beautiful medieval city, town or village with a traffic gridlock. For their first look at a possible location, the researcher or producer would often go incognito to a church service to get a feel for the community, but also to check out the double-yellow-line situation.

Sometimes a place is so perfect, in spite of apparently insurmountable parking problems, that everyone refuses to be beaten. I well remember waking up in my bedroom in a bed and breakfast in the tiny little Cornish

harbour town of Coverack to see the window darken as the BBC vans inched their way along the narrow street at dawn, complete with a police escort. It was a nail-biting moment, and an enthusiastic recording of their traditional Cornish 'Carolare' was only possible because one of *Songs of Praise*'s most indomitable technical operations managers, the late and much-missed Jack Belasco, would not say 'no'. Pub signs were taken down, tree branches were trimmed, traffic was stopped – and the *Songs of Praise* cavalcade got through.

Nowadays, however, with much more flexible recording equipment, there are fewer places beyond the reach of the BBC scanners. Ludlow in Shropshire came closest to beating the *Songs of Praise* technical team recently, with its beautiful church hemmed in by ancient buildings and accessible only by foot. In the end, however, BBC crews wriggle their way into even the most inaccessible corner. With much smaller equipment, producers and the team can now even take everything apart and pack it into suitcases. Even so, the suitcases are of the largest and most formidable variety and air passengers endeavouring to check in behind a *Songs of Praise* crew en route to a foreign location are unlucky.

When producer Chris Mann produced a programme from Turkey, just after the Gulf War, to show the work of aid agencies working with the Kurdish community on the border with northern Iraq, he set up all the equipment in his hotel room. This included a portable satellite dish which he placed on the terrace. Chris remembers the puzzled and suspicious glances he got as he and other members of the team repeatedly walked through the hotel lobby carrying large rocks to hold the dish in place against the gale-force mountain winds.

### Finishing touches

Once the *Songs of Praise* music recording is complete, singers and musicians disperse, tired but reasonably jubilant that their programme is 'in the can', and the people in Bradford were no exception.

For the producer, even with all the interviews filmed and music recorded, it is still just the halfway stage. Some music is now recorded like a pop video, one shot at a time, as was the case with Deronda K. Lewis's performance of the song 'Don't Give Up' on the Bradford programme. There can be more than 200 different shots of the locality and of the people featured and all these have to be edited together to make the final programme.

The editing begins with up to four days spent in a darkened room looking at some very sophisticated computer screens. These display all the available shots and it is possible to look at many at once. It is rather like looking at contact prints when you are getting photographs developed. They always look tremendous in their tiny little boxes.

Together with a video editor, the producer can now assemble *Songs of Praise* in any order he or she chooses. Working on such a state-of-the-art non-linear electronic editing system is in complete contrast with my own early days on the programme, when editing was a one-off chance to get it right, with two-inch-wide videotape being physically cut. Mistakes were fatal, especially if an anonymous piece of electronic tape containing the last line of a hymn verse fell under the editing machine guillotine.

Today, making a *Songs of Praise* fit the precise transmission space it is allotted on BBC1 is the source of a different sort of grief. The producer's – or sometimes the conductor's – most favourite moments always seem to be the ones that have to be edited out to save a vital minute. It wasn't always this way. In the old days the exact timing was done at the actual recording. A veteran of one of the first *Songs of Praise* programmes in 1961 remembers 'a young woman who kept appearing while we rehearsed with the cameras and firmly telling us that we would have to sing this or that hymn much faster to save ten seconds. Then it was another three seconds to be saved in the last hymn. It was a lively experience for our conductor.' As the organist on that occasion, he says that he has always accompanied hymns very briskly since that day.

By far the hardest task is the editing of a complex but vivid story of faith down to fewer than three minutes. Roger Hutchings, who edited *Songs of Praise* in the 1980s,

remembers his own first effort at a filmed interview. He had been sent to interview Metropolitan Anthony of Sourozh, the leader of the Russian Orthodox Church. Roger told Metropolitan Anthony that he had just three questions.

'What are they?' asked the archbishop, and, once Roger had explained, after a pause he replied, 'Yes, that will be possible; my answers will take about 70 minutes.'

'Thank you,' said Roger's boss when he'd finished. 'Can you quickly edit it down to five?'

In *Songs of Praise*, music has the priority, and editors always try to include more than 20 minutes of hymn-singing in each 35-minute programme. When producer David Taviner had edited his Bradford recording, he was relieved that only one verse of one hymn needed to be cut out.

Finally, at the Bradford edit, when Hugh Faupel, the editor, and Michael Wakelin, the series producer, had had a look at the finished programme, they made use of the new editing technology to change the music order, so that the familiar hymn 'Holy, holy, holy, Lord God Almighty' was nearer to the beginning. It is surprising how quickly the *Songs of Praise* audience can fade away if there isn't something they know early on. It was all done with a few double-clicks on the computer mouse and the equivalent of the 'cut and paste' familiar to anyone with a PC. They hoped they had achieved something that the audience would enjoy, a blend of the familiar with the unfamiliar.

For Harry Atkinson of Kala Sangam, the organization that brought along some Indian dancers to interpret a haunting refrain, 'The Lord is present', there was an extra bonus when the programme was shown. With this dance Harry, born and bred in Bradford and a member of the Church of England, introduced what *Songs of Praise* called 'a taste of South Asian culture'. As Harry said of Geetha, one of the beautiful dancers, 'We differ greatly, but our aim is the same.'

Watching the Bradford broadcast was Harry's former primary-school teacher, 92-year-old Winifred Wallbank. They hadn't seen each other for 50 years, and Mrs Wallbank is not a regular *Songs of Praise* viewer but had just happened to switch on. For two people at least, this edition of *Songs of Praise* had a real-life happy ending.

# Five

# Brief Encounters

## *Songs of Praise* Comes Down Your Way

On the first Sunday of 1977 many regular viewers of *Songs of Praise* must have sat up in astonishment as their favourite programme began. Instead of the sound of an opening hymn being sung over a still caption of the church hosting the edition – in this case St Mary's Parish Church, Rye – there was a short film of the famously picturesque Sussex town perched on a hill at the western edge of the Romney Marshes. There was also a signature tune, which sounded a bit like a familiar hymn tune, although nobody would be able to say which one, and it sounded as though it was being played by a pop group. As the drums and guitars faded away, Percy Sherwood, Rye's town crier, rang his bell and bellowed out words which must have been heard right across the marsh: 'O yea, O yea! Welcome to *Songs of Praise* from Rye!'

Standing next to the town crier, hands over his ears, was a very familiar TV face, but one that had never before been seen on *Songs of Praise* – Michael Barratt, the

presenter known to millions of viewers as the face of the early-evening weekday news and current-affairs programme, *Nationwide*. *Songs of Praise* had launched its biggest-ever makeover.

**New faces**

Although Michael Barratt was in Rye to introduce the first hymn, which followed only a couple of minutes later, regular viewers immediately divided into two camps. Some simply hated it. Actually – a lot hated it. The signature tune was an 'electronic jingle' that did nothing for the programme. The new set-up had completely destroyed the feeling of being part of the congregation. One viewer wrote in to say that 'getting through to the few is surely far more important than pleasing the masses and beating ITV figures'.

Some viewers, however, wrote to the *Radio Times* offering congratulations for the biggest, most important change of all that had been made to the programme: the introduction of the interviews. As one of them wrote: 'I have often wondered about the folk when the camera picks them up in the congregation. (I once saw a friend whom I had not seen for many years.) I now feel we have a little more contact with at least some of them and can think of them as individuals who live ordinary lives as I do.'

After each hymn, the camera picked out one of the singers, who then featured in a short film about their life and faith. Postman Ralph Holland delivering mail in Rye was first, remembering how, after an unhappy

watches every week, it was the turning-point: 'I have always been a selective viewer and although I was aware of *Songs of Praise* before, one programme sounded much like another to me. Now I found myself really lost in the experience; heavenly. It is so non-parsonical, and you can share the prayers from the heart of ordinary people.'

Today, many viewers associate *Songs of Praise* with the enjoyment of hearing people's stories, helping to explain why they came together for this musical celebration of

*Left*: Rye Harbour, featured in the first new-look *Songs of Praise* with interviews in 1977.

*Right*: Author and local preacher Wallace Grevatt, one of *Songs of Praise*'s most loyal viewers, at home in Brighton.

childhood, he was made very welcome by a Christian pastor and his family. That in turn had led him to the Methodist Church and he recalled one of the first hymns he had learned there: 'Love divine, all loves excelling'. At this point, viewers were transported back to the church just in time for everyone to sing 'Love divine, all loves excelling'.

Ralph Holland had completed the *Songs of Praise* revolution. He was the first of thousands to choose the hymns for each week's programme. For viewers such as Wallace Grevatt in Brighton, who still

Christian faith. In the early days, it was much harder to convince some viewers, let alone some potential interviewees.

For the first few programmes, there was only one researcher, Liz Gort. Some years later, Liz was to become my wife, but in those opening days our relationship was as colleagues, as I directed many of the film interviews while she searched the towns and villages of Britain for the people to choose the hymns.

Having read theology at Manchester College, Oxford, Liz had developed a keen interest in religious broadcasting and especially in how far the medium could go in involving viewers in an experience of worship beyond the obvious 'fly-on-the-wall' televised relay of a church service. How about the visual possibilities of the world beyond the church walls and the individual experience of faith tested by the changes and chances of life?

had the original idea of introducing viewers to the lives of the people who were in the church singing their songs of praise. He asked Ray Short, the series producer, together with producer Michael Shoesmith and Bill Nicholson, a film director, to make a pilot for a new-look *Songs of Praise*.

Bill is now a well-known writer, best-known

*Below*: **Before the interview Pam Rhodes gets to know the members of one of the world's most famous choirs, the Vienna Boys' Choir.**

*Right*: **Aled Jones prepares to interview the warden of the New Room (John Wesley's Chapel) in Bristol, none other than fellow broadcaster Frank Topping.**

The head of the BBC's religious television department at that time was Peter Armstrong, an immensely gifted radio and TV producer who in the 1970s had innovated many new approaches to religious television with programmes such as *This is the Day*, *Heart of the Matter* and the highly regarded documentary programme *Everyman* which, like *Songs of Praise*, is a mainstay of the department's output to this day. Peter had

for his work on *Shadowlands*, the award-winning film depicting the love and pain in the life of C.S. Lewis, and most recently he was one of the screen-writers of the Hollywood blockbuster *Gladiator*. In those days he was a comparative novice, and was sent with a film crew to Godmanchester in Huntingdonshire, where – I think unwittingly – in the wartime documentary style of Humphrey Jennings he filmed the daily round... over and over again.

While Bill filmed her, one woman made pot after pot after pot of jam and marmalade, all the while musing about her faith; another lady swept, polished and dusted the empty church until dust practically had to be imported. It was a long time before Peter Armstrong felt the team had the essence of what he had in mind and the inhabitants of Godmanchester must have felt they were earning sainthood over their jam-boilers and dustpans and brushes.

Meanwhile Liz had talked her way into a job in the department, and because her thinking had been much along the same lines as Peter's plans for the new-style *Songs of Praise*, she was teamed up with Ray to work as the first researcher. She remembers the first team meeting chaired by Ray when he had to convince the other producers from the different regions and nations that the new idea would run and run like *Songs of Praise*. They had many doubts and objections. Wouldn't we quickly run out of saintly vergers, bell-ringers, flower arrangers and the like, with interviewees becoming boring and monotonous once the novelty wore off? After almost 25 years, however, the novelty has not worn off to judge by *Songs of Praise*'s regular weekly audience of as many as six million viewers.

Back in 1976, once the pilot for a new *Songs of Praise* was approved, I replaced Bill Nicholson and began to direct the films for each programme. To me, even the most ordinary activity filmed sympathetically could make good television. I had had a good deal of practice filming Britain

at work for schools' TV, and I think I had faced the ultimate challenge when I had to make the mechanical production of a well-known chocolate bar – one which had fruit and nuts mixed into it – appear so stimulating that it could be chosen as a career.

I am glad that Michael Barratt and I filmed steel-making in Ebbw Vale, an exciting scenario worthy of William Blake and now a historical archive. One of my film sequences nearly finished us all off, however. We were filming a Christian gentleman who was the owner-operator of the last horse-drawn refuse cart in Britain. Of course, we had to film the interview on the dustcart with Michael Barratt and our subject travelling around the town. Michael, wearing a new sheepskin-lined car coat, looked warily at me as he unwillingly hauled himself up onto the cart next to his interviewee. As they talked, the horse pulled them up a steep hill through the town's one-way system. The film crew and I were hanging off the tailboard of a Land Rover just ahead of them. It was a wonderful interview until we reached the hymn choice, at which point neither Michael nor his interviewee could remember what it was. Disaster. In those days we had an absolute rule that the person interviewed must name the hymn and the tune – that they had chosen. Nothing for it but we had to make our way back through the one-way system to the start at the bottom of the hill. And so we did – three more times before both words and tune were

Michael Barratt filming the opening of the 1977 *Songs of Praise* from Dulwich and Herne Hill with producer Ray Short (left) and top film cameraman A.A. Englander.

announced correctly. So fascinated was one shopkeeper by this regular and increasingly ridiculous procession around the one-way system that she rushed out as it passed on 'Take 4' and offered Michael a huge cream doughnut. Grateful, but feeling obliged to eat it, Michael took a bite, at which point its creamy contents sprayed all over his new coat. Fortunately I could not hear Michael's words of rebuke to his director, but I shall not forget the look in his eyes. In case you are anxious, the horse had a very happy day.

Geoffrey Wheeler, trailing the aura of the perfect schoolmaster from his long association with *Top of the Form*, had been presenting *Songs of Praise* for some time before the new style began, and I suspect he holds the record for the longest ever association with it. He was hugely popular wherever we went, and a lot of interviewees were far less alarmed at the prospect of being interviewed by him than by the rather formidable Michael Barratt. I have never forgotten the time when an elderly lady who made cardboard boxes took Geoffrey to her heart. She lived in a street where parking was absolutely impossible, so I had to leave Geoffrey in her company while the film crew and I found somewhere for the vehicles. By the time we returned, Geoffrey was well into a huge north-country tea and he had learned everything there was to know about the intricacies of cardboard-box manufacture. Geoffrey helped her through a delightful interview, but only after she had absolutely insisted on our filming her giving the surprisingly complex description of her work. 'I owe it to you all', she said, 'to get it just right for *Songs of Praise*.'

One of the tips for researchers looking for the very best interviews for the programme is to find the people who would never dream of putting themselves forward. Sometimes the more unwilling they are to be filmed the better, since this is often evidence of an unsung hero. This has been particularly the case with programmes coming from Northern Ireland. Over many years of conflict highlighted daily in the news, *Songs of Praise* has set out to tell the stories of Christians of all denominations who faithfully help to keep normal life going in abnormal circumstances. There have been many stories of kindliness to strangers and 'doing' rather than talking about reconciliation. And, interestingly enough, bringing different denominations together for *Songs of Praise* in Northern Ireland has never been as difficult as it can sometimes be in other parts of Britain.

Now and again, watching a *Songs of Praise* interview leads to the start of something big for a viewer. At the end of 1988 Judy Birchall, a family solicitor living in Cheshire, was watching *Songs of Praise* from Nottingham. There was an interview with Mary Lower, a member of the United Reformed Church, who was running a family contact centre where separated and divorced couples could meet and where young children caught up in marital disputes could play in a safe and friendly environment.

Judy was so impressed that she decided to set up a similar centre at her own local Baptist church in Altrincham. It was a life-changing decision for her, and the centre has gone from strength to strength. May 2001 marked the 10th anniversary of the National Association of Child Contact Centres, and now there are more than 300 in Britain. Yet recently, when Judy watched a recording of that original 1988 *Songs of Praise*, she was amazed to discover how short Mary Lower's interview had been: 'I can't believe how little there was actually to do with contact centres. Yet how profound an impression it made on me.'

Perhaps above all, stories of courage and faith in the face of adversity have always played a big part in *Songs of Praise*. Former

Ecumenical putting at St Andrew's. Producer Maurice Maguire films Dr James Simpson, former moderator of the General Assembly of the Church of Scotland, competing against Bishop Joseph Devine, Roman Catholic bishop of Motherwell. Bishop Michael Henley of the Scottish Episcopal Church is the umpire.

editor Roger Hutchings remembers viewing Martin Bashir's interview with Jane Renouf, filmed in a programme from the Lake District. Jane's son had died of leukaemia a year earlier and Jane was later to write a book, *Jimmy*, about the whole experience of grief and loss. For Roger, it was the most impressive interview that he can remember: 'There was not an "easy" line in it. Jane had no sense then of her son having gone to heaven. We were hearing a woman going through agonies still. She was just not prepared to come out with an easy assurance of the love of God. And yet she was prepared to take her part in *Songs of Praise*.'

Even with a lifetime's experience of ministry in the Methodist Church, Roger says there were plenty of occasions when he was reduced to tears while viewing the filmed interviews at the editing stage: 'It can be quite hard to follow the Spirit of Jesus in a postmodern age of pic 'n' mix faith, but I think that's what *Songs of Praise* at its best shows ordinary people doing.'

**Almost beyond words**

Perhaps the most painful test of faith that I myself have witnessed came in the few days in March 1997 that I spent in Dunblane after the terrible shooting in the town's primary school. Although I was responsible for all BBC Scotland's religious broadcasting, it was in collaboration with another *Songs of Praise* editor, Helen Alexander, that we were to make a special *Songs of Praise* for the following Sunday, which, by the cruellest of ironies, was Mothering Sunday.

On the day before transmission, Helen and I, together with Sally Magnusson, filmed an interview in a little room overlooking Dunblane Cathedral. Among the many shattered people in Dunblane at that time were the Reverend Bryan Owen, an Anglican

Her Majesty the Queen leaves Dunblane Cathedral on Mothering Sunday 1997 after a private meeting with relatives of the dead and injured children. A special *Songs of Praise* from the town was transmitted a few minutes later.

priest working for Scottish Churches House, and his wife Kathy, a Church of Scotland minister who was working in Stirling Royal Infirmary. Their four-year-old son, Stewart, was a pupil in Dunblane Primary School. After an agonizing wait, they finally heard that he was safe.

By an odd coincidence I had met Bryan almost exactly 10 years before, when we both became involved in another appalling tragedy, the Zeebrugge ferry disaster. I had the job then of producing religious broadcasts for the ITV region serving Dover, where so many people waited in the same sort of agony for news. I was producing the television coverage of a service of national mourning. Bryan had spent many days sitting alongside relatives and friends in their grief. I am sure that we both hoped we would never meet again in such circumstances. Nevertheless, here we were

meeting again at another time of profound tragedy, and Bryan and Kathy were among only a handful of people we felt able to approach for a programme that has perhaps been *Songs of Praise*'s greatest test. During the interview there were to be long pauses as Bryan and Kathy took it in turns to speak:

*Bryan: Somehow, this is not a time for words; our minds can't take in the words. It's the human comfort that we can give each other that seems to have been what's most necessary.*

*Kathy: Being in the places where people hurt most is the only place to be. And you're not offering anything other than basic human qualities of love; and I have to say that in the town there has been a tremendous spirit of love and I think a spirit of gentleness and kindness and goodness, because people are just reaching out to one another – so that's undergirded everything that I've done.*

*I've felt really and truly held together by the love of other folk and it's come through cards and it's come in practical ways, but I think you would find the folk in the town would say that it's there and you know that it's there and because it's there you can function.*

*Bryan: I've been holding onto Psalm 139 these last few days and in that psalm, at the end, there are angry words that the psalmist says to God. What that psalm has said to me is that it's all right to be angry. I'm angry for all the people in Dunblane who've suffered. I'm angry that this should have happened, this violation of the sanctity of a school.*

*Kathy (reading from her Bible some verses of Psalm 139):*

*O Lord, you have searched me,*
*   and you know me.*
*You know when I sit and when I rise;*
*   you perceive my thoughts from afar...*
*Where can I go from your Spirit?*
*   Where can I flee from your presence?*
*If I go up to the heavens, you are there;*
*   if I make my bed in the depths, you are there...*
*even the darkness will not be dark to you;*
*   the night will shine like the day,*
*   for darkness is as light to you...*
*If only you would slay the wicked, O God!...*
*They speak of you with evil intent;*
*   your adversaries misuse your name...*
*I have nothing but hatred for them;*
*   I count them my enemies.*
*Search me, O God, and know my heart;*
*   test me and know my anxious thoughts.*
*See if there is any offensive way in me,*
*   and lead me in the way everlasting.*

Psalm 139:1–2, 7–8, 12, 19–20, 22–24

*Bryan: We're in a Good Friday experience at*
*the moment, an experience of bereavement. In*
*our own family life we've been in that situation*
*before, and we know that we have to come out*
*into resurrection. And because it's happened*
*before, because God has been with us through*
*dark moments and brought us through, we*
*trust that God will be with us in these dark*
*moments and will bring us through.*

*Kathy: It's one thing to know the theory of*
*resurrection and quite another to live through*
*it. And it's not just the people in Dunblane who*
*are doing that. There are people each and every*
*day who have to live through the dark moments*
*and then eventually feel the light coming again*
*and that's the universal experience... it has to*
*be lived through to be understood.*

A verse from Percy Dearmer's hymn,
'Jesus, good above all other', was sung
immediately after Bryan and Kathy's
interview:

*Jesus, who our sorrows bearest,*
*   all our thoughts and hopes thou sharest,*
*thou to us the truth declarest;*
*   help us all thy truth to hear.*

# Six

# It'll Be All Right on the Night

## Why *Songs of Praise* Has Never Been a Disaster Movie

'Y ou'll have to stop the recording, my camera's gone through the floor!'

'Excuse me, Mister, your wires are on fire!'

Over the years of *Songs of Praise*, many producers have kept the congregation happy while some technical preparation is completed by describing occasions when – for another programme – it certainly was *not* 'all right on the night'. We have all had our share of near disaster, even of actual disaster. In hindsight these accidents seem funny and can raise a laugh. At the time, however, they felt like the end of the world.

*Songs of Praise* is very demure when it comes to *Auntie's Bloomers*, the BBC programme presented by Terry Wogan in which the moments where filming has gone ridiculously wrong are shown. *Songs of Praise*

has always kept a dignified silence, as though on a religious programme things could not possibly ever go awry. On reflection, I think I have experienced more than my fair share of incidents over the years.

**Don't panic, chaps**

During one recording, while parked in a cathedral close, former series producer Ray Short remembers hearing a gentle but insistent tapping on the door of the mobile control room. Everyone was busy and ignored it. Finally someone opened the door of the scanner to reveal what Ray describes as a 'little old lady, who was slowly vanishing behind the haze of smoke from burning cables under the van'.

I was helping Ray with a harvest festival programme from the parish church of Kidlington in Oxfordshire, when the hymn-singing abruptly stopped and people collapsed into laughter. I turned round just in time to see a camera and its operator sinking slowly through the grating in the floor of the chancel. My heart sank with them, but I had to admire the generous and unworried response of the vicar and the churchwardens, who took the view that 'the show must go on' as we all teamed up to haul the camera back up out of its hole. Even though the BBC is well insured and always puts right any damage – which is only very rarely done – it was not a moment to savour. But one or two participants told me later that it had made their evening.

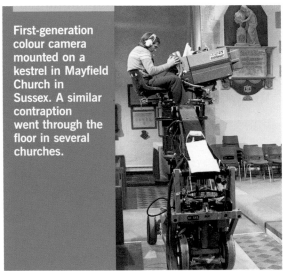

First-generation colour camera mounted on a kestrel in Mayfield Church in Sussex. A similar contraption went through the floor in several churches.

Not so long ago, *Songs of Praise* came – without incident – from St Barnabas's, Dulwich, where the congregation was celebrating the completion of a brand-new church replacing a Victorian building that had gone up in flames. Fortunately, this tragedy had nothing to do with *Songs of Praise*, but there must have been many there who remembered an earlier *Songs of Praise*, recorded in St Barnabas's one evening in the hot summer of 1976. Just as everyone had assembled for the rehearsal, all the TV lights went out – and stayed out. I rushed to the pulpit and assured everyone

with totally unfounded confidence that we would soon be starting. In the meantime, they would all enjoy a final practice, wouldn't they?

Outside, the technical operations director was determined to reassure me. 'It's all right,' he said cheerfully, 'the generator has collapsed completely. But there's another one on the way!' He smiled at me optimistically.

He was right, and luckily the other generator was at nearby Crystal Palace, only a few miles away. It wouldn't take long to arrive. I returned in triumph to the church, where in the gloom Canon Perry, the vicar of St Barnabas's, was looking extremely worried and pessimistic. He was right.

An hour later, the technical director informed me that he had further good news: 'Another generator is on its way!' It was coming from a distant part of West London around one of the most notorious of traffic jammers, the South Circular Road.

'Why hasn't the generator arrived from Crystal Palace?' I asked in despair.

'It is doing a live *Sportsnight* on BBC1,' he admitted.

I set off back with more implausible explanations for my assembled talent of singers, who by now were generating their own Dunkirk spirit. They had stayed loyally in their pews for almost two hours on a boiling hot summer night, and we had achieved nothing.

I told them the truth. The cavalry was on its way, but we needed a miracle of Red Sea proportions to clear the traffic. 'However,' I said, in the palest imitation of Jesus' miracles with loaves and fishes, 'I shall return shortly with provisions, South London style.' It was before the days of the takeaway, so I had to fall on the mercy of a local pub. I said I wanted everything, absolutely everything, that they had got. They had fizzy drinks and crisps. I set out with 500 cans of drink, a mountain of crisps and the only two can-openers that could be found. Back at the

church there was a huge cheer, especially from the children. But with only two can-openers it must have been the slowest refreshment service ever to take place in St Barnabas's.

We started recording three hours late, just after 10 p.m. It was to be an extraordinarily energetic *Songs of Praise*. Somehow the singers found a new lease of life, although I am sure it wasn't thanks to the refreshments. With the new generator in place – but, because it was a much smaller one, still only able to light half the church – we romped through the hymns and no one – not singers, camera crew or even the director

*Left*: Creating a snowy Victorian street scene in Brighton on a warm evening is unwise.

*Right*: Producer Simon Hammond realizes that he has overdone the smoke effect in Iona Abbey.

– made a single mistake. Depending on how you were feeling by then, it was either ironic or uplifting that one of the hymns we sang that night was 'Lead, kindly Light'.

In the 1990s, it was another crystal palace to which, as producer, I chose to go to record an Advent *Songs of Praise*. We assembled a huge choir in the elegant but then rather dilapidated surroundings of the

People's Palace on Glasgow Green. It is a quite enormous glass conservatory and, complete with a huge array of palms and exotic trees, it is the nearest thing to the original 1857 Great Exhibition building. We were there for two nights. Choirs from the Roman Catholic archdiocese amassed in front of a rostrum where young musicians were ready to accompany the singing.

On our first evening, a huge gale was blowing. The most vital parts of the roof over the orchestra vanished into the night.

'It'll be all right tomorrow,' said the conductor; 'the wind is dropping.'

He was right. Next evening in the still night air, with not a breath of wind, the rain fell steadily, searching for every way into the People's Palace. It seemed as if the musicians in particular were the targets for jets of water squirting down first into brass instruments and then onto the violins.

'This electronic organ will blow up if the rain gets in,' said the director cheerfully as we tried to mop up the young musicians.

Many of the choir members must have been present at a previous *Songs of Praise* recorded in a thunderstorm at the Glasgow Garden Festival, after which the cleaners had done particularly good business. This time, they had come prepared for they had all

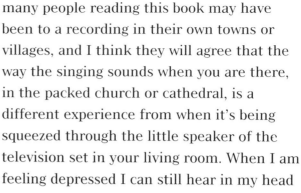

*Left: Summer Praise* from Edinburgh Castle in 1993. The producer was convinced it would be a stormy night for the 3,500 singers but it was a perfect evening.

*Below:* Squeezing in a speedy recording of *Songs of Praise* on the 18th tee of the Old Course before the Open begins.

many people reading this book may have been to a recording in their own towns or villages, and I think they will agree that the way the singing sounds when you are there, in the packed church or cathedral, is a different experience from when it's being squeezed through the little speaker of the television set in your living room. When I am feeling depressed I can still hear in my head Dan Feiten's Communion hymn, 'Seed, scattered and sown', which I heard for the first time that night in Glasgow. It looks to the day when all churches shall be one. It's very hard to explain, but in the People's Palace that night, it was almost as though we were surrounded by the seed, scattered and sown:

brought umbrellas. For the cameramen, it was a very strange evening. No one could guess where the next jet of water would land, so the only shots possible in the final rehearsal were of massed umbrellas diving this way and that to avoid the deluge. Amazingly, there is no evidence at all of the tempest in the final edited recording and, equally amazingly, I think the only person to completely avoid all the downpours was Cardinal Thomas Winning.

That evening was wonderful in a way, partly because it was so hilarious, but mainly because, as so often on *Songs of Praise*, the singing made up for everything. I suppose

*Seed, scattered and sown,*
*Wheat, gathered and grown,*
*Break, broken and shared as one,*
*The living Bread of God.*

*Vine, fruit of the land,*
*Wine, work of our hands,*
*One cup that is shared by all;*
*The Living Cup, the Living Bread of God.*

*Is not the bread we break,*
*A sharing in our Lord?*
*Is not the cup we bless,*
*The blood of Christ out-poured?*

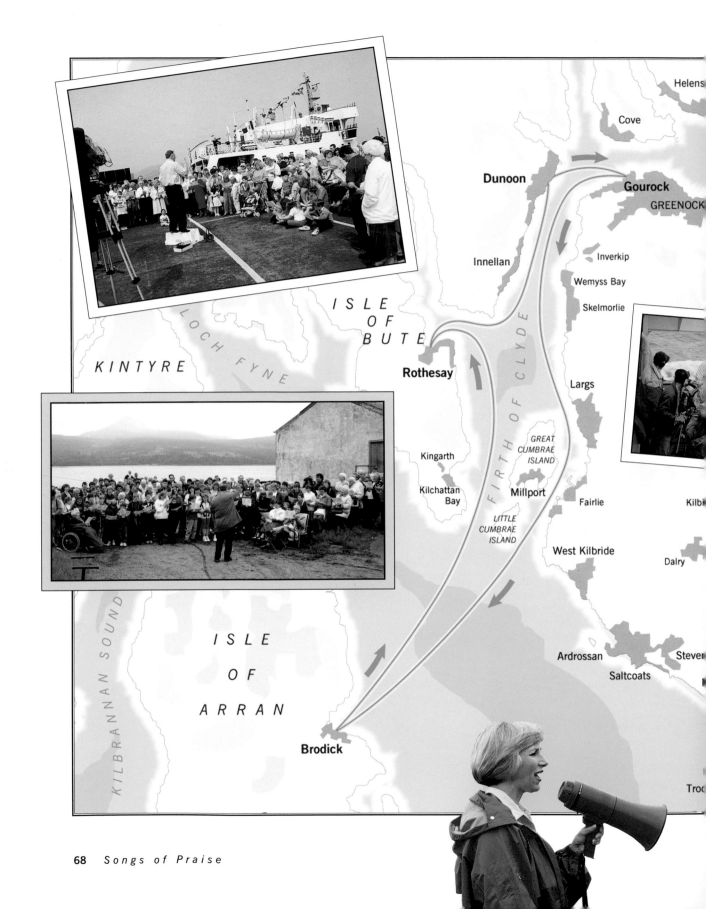

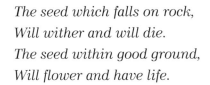

## FERRY DOWN THE CLYDE

*Songs of Praise* 'doon the watter' celebrated the tradition of a cruise on the Clyde. Members of the Toad Choir sang and visited three of the most popular holiday spots in one very busy day in summer 1993.

*Far left, top*: A quick call at Rothesay, Isle of Bute, to share a hymn with members of the town's churches under Ian McRorie's baton.

*Far left, bottom*: Braving the drizzle at Brodick, Isle of Arran.

*Middle*: Pam Rhodes interviews conductor Ian McRorie en route to the Isle of Arran.

*Below, left*: Mobile control van and outside-broadcast equipment laid out with military precision on Cal Mac's M.V. Jupiter.

*Below, right*: Final hymn sung on the pier at Dunoon on the Cowal Peninsula.

*The seed which falls on rock,*
*Will wither and will die.*
*The seed within good ground,*
*Will flower and have life.*

*As wheat upon the hills,*
*Was gathered and was grown,*
*So may the Church of God,*
*Be gathered into one.*

Directors often ask everyone to sing a hymn again, sometimes more than once, as anyone who has taken part in *Songs of Praise* knows. However, directors are quite resistant to repeating a hymn if it has looked and sounded good to them. But sometimes the need for a retake is hard to explain, especially when the person asking for it is the producer who is in the church, where he or she can be heard by everyone. That was my experience in another troubled recording, which began with a key member of the team, the floor manager – whose job it is to look after the performers

Kilmarnock

in the church – remaining sound asleep in his hotel room. Suffice it to say that the floor manager, who is no longer around, had been celebrating. So I took on his duties, liaising with the director.

As a hymn was being sung with great fervour (I think it was 'Great is thy faithfulness'), the camera closed in on the person who had chosen it. Sound and pictures were perfect... except that I noticed a tooth fly out of our interviewee's mouth just as the camera zoomed in for his close-up. Had my eyes deceived me? I walked gingerly down the nave as the singers sat down to hear the verdict. There certainly was a tooth on the floor under a pew, but no one moved to pick it up.

'I am not going to ask them to sing that again,' said the director testily into my ear-piece, 'unless you give me a really good reason.'

'I can't and you must,' I said, wishing that, like the camera in Kidlington, I could sink through the floor. In the end, it was another lovely programme, but although *Songs of Praise* has been back to that particular church, I have kept away.

I suspect my colleagues were beginning to wonder if I was as accident prone as the hapless Frank Spencer played by Michael Crawford in *Some Mothers Do 'Ave 'Em*. There was the time when a Royal Navy frigate, carefully repainted for *Songs of Praise* on one side only, steamed off while the Royal Marine band played 'Sunset' – only to lose all power seconds later.

I came closest to disaster, trying as a friendly rival to outwit *Songs of Praise*'s producers, when, working with Harry Secombe on *Highway*, I created an intricate sequence on a preserved railway. The plan was for Harry to sing 'Look for the silver lining' while his own private steam train arrived, and then he was to board the train and be carried away into the sunset. Harry had to stroll nonchalantly through a musical interlude, board the train and close the door, singing his final verse as he vanished from sight. All was going perfectly. The train arrived, the musical interlude arrived, Harry reached out nonchalantly to open the door, but it wouldn't open. Harry kept calm. He moved with studied elegance along the platform, trying one door handle after another – but they were all locked. Everyone collapsed in hysterics. Who was the well-meaning railway person who had locked the carriage doors for security purposes just before that final take?

Small diplomatic problems occur frequently in a programme in which so many people from the community want to take part. These can blow up to near volcanic proportions if a local newspaper gets to hear what's going on. A south-coast evening paper headlined a mass walk-out by disapproving singers after a TV rehearsal. I was horrified. I rushed nervously around trying to reconcile the singers and discover what the matter was. But who and where were they? I eventually discovered that one single individual had taken a dim view because they had been asked to sit in a different pew. It wasn't quite such a good story as a mass walk-out, but it touched a raw nerve. After all, some faithful souls have always sat in the same pew all their lives. It is their pew, even though pew rents are a thing of the distant past.

Whenever *Songs of Praise* comes to town, some of the host church's oldest supporters will turn up to stake out their seats around mid-afternoon. With their sandwiches and a flask of tea, they 'shall not be moved', even if a fidgety primary-school choir hems them in. I remember one early programme when it was just as if a Grandma Giles had come to life in the centre of the front row. She sat bang in the middle of where the conductor wanted the trebles to sit. Eventually, huffing and puffing and thoroughly put out she moved elsewhere and kindly camera people ensured that the director included a shot of her.

Whenever Geoffrey Wheeler came to the *Songs of Praise* recording he liked to be unobtrusive. On one occasion he was trying as usual to slip into his place by a side door in a big parish church in the north of England.

'Nay! Nay!' said the verger who had turned out to meet him in his finest robes. 'Thou'll follow me in a nice orderly way.'

So Geoffrey had to wait until the mayor and corporation in their chains of office were in place and then he was led by the verger, proudly bearing his wand of office, right down the centre aisle of the church to the waiting cameras. Fortunately, as a layreader of the Church of England, Geoffrey was able to carry it off with good grace; but the director, Stuart Cross, later to be bishop of Blackburn, was greatly entertained, sitting in the scanner watching it all on camera, to see his friend and colleague struggling to disguise his embarrassment as he was regally 'sticked' to his place.

Perhaps the closest *Songs of Praise* ever

'Another take and I shall be under water.' Alan Titchmarsh completes his last link on the Sand of Iona as the crew enjoys a glorious midsummer Hebridean night in 1991.

came to real disaster was at Christmas in 1969. The previous Christmas Ray Short had made a programme with Cliff Richard at Holy Trinity, Manchester, along with a very popular folk group called The Settlers and a large group of young people. It was a great success and reached a huge audience. The following year it was decided to repeat it on the Sunday before Christmas. A few days before transmission Ray Short discovered that the whole recording had been erased. His programme no longer existed. Although it had already been transmitted once, it was a real catastrophe as the programme had been announced in the *Radio Times* and, because of Cliff's popularity, the BBC would look ridiculous if the reason for its failure to appear became known.

After the initial shock had passed, Ray got to work trying to remount the programme. Cliff said that his schedule was impossible that week. He could not possibly get back to Manchester where the original programme had been made, but he did offer to go anywhere in the London area, as long as he could first take a Bible class finishing at 5 p.m. So that was fine. All Ray had to do now – in four days – was find an outside-broadcasting unit and technical team from nowhere, not forgetting to find a church prepared to do an unplanned *Songs of Praise* 'live' on the Sunday before Christmas.

This was how Ray Short came to meet the Reverend Richard Bewes, now based at All Souls', Langham Place, London. Richard Bewes took up the challenge, alerting his congregation at St Peter's, Harold Wood, that their annual Christmas carol service was going to take a rather dramatic form that year, and in front of a larger audience than John Wesley had preached to in his entire life. He invited them to turn out in force for a one-and-only rehearsal on Sunday afternoon, and they would be on air that evening. Cliff Richard not only agreed to sing some solos, but also to introduce all the hymns. By 5.15 p.m., just an hour and a half before the programme was to go out on the air, the church was lit, the scripts written, everything and everyone was ready... but no Cliff. Minutes later, however, he turned up and not long afterwards everyone was live on BBC1, watched by almost 20 million viewers.

Most of the singers had never even heard the 'Calypso Carol' before and had to learn it from scratch that afternoon. But that was to be one of the memorable highlights for many of the hundreds of viewers who telephoned Richard Bewes that night. Cliff was, as ever, a star. And what Richard Bewes later described as four days of 'Trojan-like activity' set a *Songs of Praise* audience record that was unbeaten for years afterwards. And, after all, it was all right on the night.

# 'Now You'll Only Get This Once...'

## The Stranger Excursions of *Songs of Praise*

From the hundreds of letters sent to the *Songs of Praise* production office every week, it is clear that there are many different opinions about what ingredients go to make up the perfect programme. One thing that nearly everyone seems to agree about, however, is that uplifting music and beautiful scenery make Sunday-evening viewing an enjoyable experience. With some stunning shots of the Highlands of Scotland an edition in January 2001 looking at the real life behind the fictional world of BBC1's *The Monarch of the Glen* achieved one of the highest audiences for years. A week or so before, *Songs of Praise* came from inner-city Salford, and was introduced by a local actress, Anne Kirkbride, better known as Deirdre from ITV's *Coronation Street*. It showed the resurrection of the former docklands area,

and also attracted a very large audience. But when you can't always have beautiful scenery or famous names, what is the secret ingredient that makes people still want to go on watching after 40 years?

Well. How about a high-speed train? Or the RAF's Red Arrows display team?

For Chris Mann, producer of many memorable programmes, the way to success is to enthuse choirs, musicians and congregations to join him in making *Songs of Praise* out of some of the most unlikely and improbable ingredients that only his wild imagination is capable of. (He believes that there will be a *Songs of Praise* from the moon in his lifetime.) Some of Chris's best programmes have come from a chance meeting with fellow enthusiasts susceptible to his original ideas who somehow find themselves responding, 'Why not?'

**Musical chairs on the Wesley Express**

Roger Hutchings, former editor of the programme, described to me this nightmarish preamble to the most challenging recording of his career.

A *Songs of Praise* planning meeting is being held in a gloomy hall in the great Victorian-gothic pile known as 'The Chambers' fronting London's St Pancras Station. Chris Mann is in one of his most creative moods as he circles around bemused senior managers from British Rail, telling them about his latest wheeze. A chance meeting with one of them, David Maidment, at his local church in Barnes, has set Chris thinking about how *Songs of Praise* might celebrate Methodism – which he has heard described as the 'travelling religion'.

At the time David, Chris's new Methodist acquaintance, held the post of British Rail's punctuality officer, so Chris thought that he was just the man to organize a travelling *Songs of Praise* using a train to visit the most famous places associated with John and Charles Wesley. In fact, David himself had already had the beginnings of an excellent idea to raise funds for the Railway Children (a charity devoted to helping homeless children) by hiring a train. For Chris, though, this was just the start.

'Surely you all would agree that it could be the most magical of moments', he said, still circling, spectacles agleam, 'if not one but three trains roar out of St Pancras, one after the other, all

**A WESLEYAN TOUR**

1988 was the 250th anniversary of John and Charles Wesley's conversion. Let the trains take the strain as *Songs of Praise* travels to Wesley country.

*Top right*: Chris Mann tries to organize camera crew, band and choir into a high-speed hymn recording.

*Right*: Methodist choirs realize that Chris Mann expects brilliant harmonies at 100 m.p.h.

*Far right*: Chris Mann at home in 2001 with his cherished souvenir.

*Below*: Powerful, sparkling-clean Class 47 diesels ready to leave St Pancras.

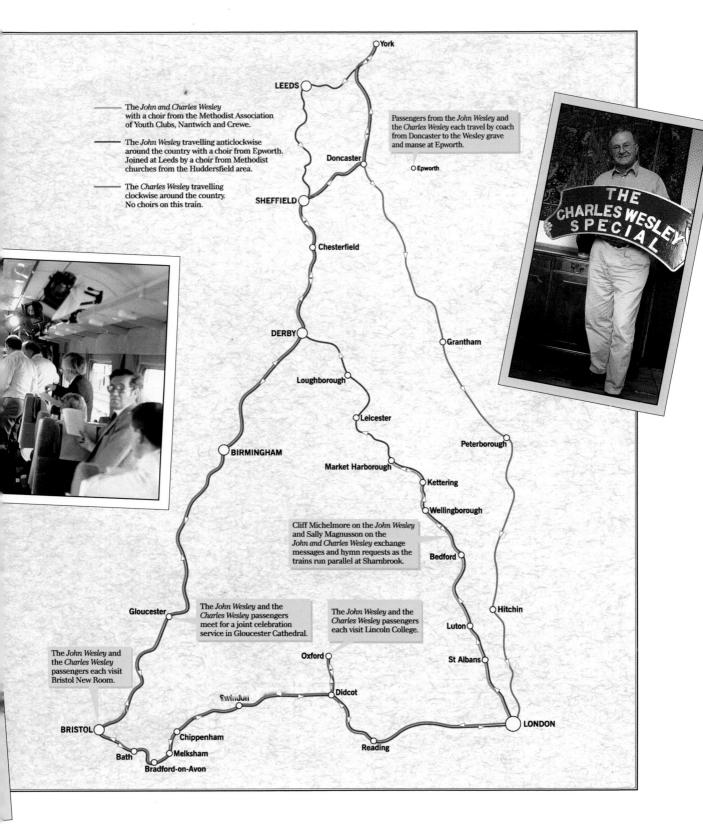

The *John and Charles Wesley* with a choir from the Methodist Association of Youth Clubs, Nantwich and Crewe.

The *John Wesley* travelling anticlockwise around the country with a choir from Epworth. Joined at Leeds by a choir from Methodist churches from the Huddersfield area.

The *Charles Wesley* travelling clockwise around the country. No choirs on this train.

Passengers from the *John Wesley* and the *Charles Wesley* each travel by coach from Doncaster to the Wesley grave and manse at Epworth.

Cliff Michelmore on the *John Wesley* and Sally Magnusson on the *John and Charles Wesley* exchange messages and hymn requests as the trains run parallel at Sharnbrook.

The *John Wesley* and the *Charles Wesley* passengers meet for a joint celebration service in Gloucester Cathedral.

The *John Wesley* and the *Charles Wesley* passengers each visit Lincoln College.

The *John Wesley* and the *Charles Wesley* passengers each visit Bristol New Room.

York
LEEDS
Doncaster
Epworth
SHEFFIELD
Chesterfield
DERBY
Grantham
Loughborough
Leicester
Peterborough
Market Harborough
BIRMINGHAM
Kettering
Wellingborough
Bedford
Hitchin
Gloucester
Luton
St Albans
Oxford
Didcot
Swindon
LONDON
BRISTOL
Chippenham
Bath
Melksham
Reading
Bradford-on-Avon

packed with singers, their voices echoing across the huge station roof as they sing "O for a thousand tongues to sing" to the great tune "Lyngham"?'

'What a prospect,' Chris went on to an assembled row of blank and frightened faces. For these were the people charged with keeping ordinary train services up to the mark, a far from easy task at the best of times, who were now being asked to put on this extra trinity of trains to carry *Songs of Praise* choirs off to all the towns and villages associated with the Wesleys. To make things even more complicated, the trains were to be called the *John Wesley*, the *Charles Wesley*, and the *John and Charles Wesley*.

There was to be even more *Songs of Praise* magic in his plan. Chris had discovered that on the bank up to Sharnbrook on the old Midland main line in Bedfordshire, two express trains could run in parallel. What an opportunity! Presenter Cliff Michelmore travelling in the *John Wesley* special could liaise with Sally Magnusson sitting with the driver of the high-speed train named the *John and Charles Wesley*. As the two trains ascended the bank side by side, choirs and a good part of a brass band in the *John Wesley* would be ready to sing the hymn choice of the driver of the *John and Charles Wesley*. Chris had even located a Methodist driver who wanted to say that with the *John Wesley* pushing and the *Charles Wesley* pulling, then truly 'all things would be working for Christ'.

'Let me show you how that will work,' said Chris to the British Rail managers. 'Can you now rearrange your chairs into two parallel rows? That's right. One row will imagine themselves as the *John Wesley* and the other the *John and Charles Wesley*. Here I am, the driver, in this row and my colleague Roger with you over there is ready to conduct the singing. And, see, we are all facing the same way!' No one can recall whether Chris added, 'And all singing from the same hymn-sheet.'

After Chris had demonstrated his novel approach to musical chairs, 'They must have been certain that we were completely mad,' remembers Roger Hutchings. But a few weeks later, with absolutely impeccable timing, the two trains ran in parallel on Sharnbrook Summit. At St Pancras, driver Peter, assisted by the Reverend Rupert Davies, president of that year's Methodist Conference, had helped to unveil a shiny new nameplate for his high-speed diesel. Then a huge choir, on the platform and in the three trains, complete with presenter Roger Royle, sang 'O for a thousand tongues to sing'. Then the three trains roared off.

With destinations Oxford, Bristol and Doncaster (for Epworth), every *Songs of Praise* director in the department was in action. Such was the punctuality of the trains that Roger Hutchings, filming an MAYC (Methodist Association of Youth Clubs) choir singing 'Jesus Christ is a picture of holiness', only finished shooting seconds before a choir alighted from the *John and Charles Wesley* arriving exactly on time at Bedford. Later he confessed to Chris Mann that he had forgotten to film one of Sally Magnusson's camera introductions until after the train had arrived at its destination so Sally had had to do the link on a stationary train, being pushed and pulled by Roger, to make it look as if she was swaying around on a moving train.

So crowds of exuberant Methodists sang their way around Britain in the footsteps of the Wesleys. Seeing a tape of this *Songs of Praise* more than a dozen years later, hearing Peter the driver choosing 'Jesu, lover of my soul' and watching the choir leap into action on board the other train to sing it for him – all just as Chris Mann had planned it – it is difficult to believe that behind the scenes any number of serious, professional railwaymen and television engineers were tearing their hair out to bring all this to the screen. Sally Magnusson's greeting to Cliff Michelmore as their trains met in the heart of the English shires – 'Ahoy there, Cliff!' – perfectly catches the spirit of this unbelievably crazy but ultimately successful and joyful venture.

**Cue the Red Arrows**

No witnesses have come forward to describe the planning meeting that began another Chris Mann spectacular. The idea, in short, was a live programme from RAF Scampton that looked back to the Second World War Dambusters sortie. It was to open with the top Red Arrows display team swooping down out of the sky to arrive at the precise moment when the singers and an RAF band were giving their all in an aircraft hanger to a setting of Psalm 46: 'God is our refuge and strength' set to the tune of the Dambusters' March.

'It won't work, Chris,' Sally Magnusson remembers saying, as she rehearsed what was to be her live introduction from the edge of the runway. Her link was being timed to finish with the dramatic arrival of the jet planes and their coloured plumes of smoke. Chris was exuding his customary confidence, having persuaded the BBC news that it must not overrun by a single second, which is in itself some feat. They ended spot on. Previewing his shots through the cameras, Chris saw tiny specks in the sky heading straight towards Sally, rather sooner than he had calculated. She hadn't started her link. Seconds later – no one heard whether Chris did say 'cue the Red Arrows', 'cue Sally' or indeed cue anyone – they had already arrived. They swooped down over a totally inaudible Sally, who smiled rather desperately as she then vanished from sight in clouds of multicoloured smoke.

All would seem to have been lost, but in an instant the choir and band were on-screen singing perfectly, the din had gone and by the end of the first verse the Red Arrows were perfectly synchronizing their famous barrel-roll with the hymn. It looked like a miracle. But it wasn't. What had saved the day? Chris had secretly recorded the last choir rehearsal, which quite often is the best performance of all. So *Songs of Praise* viewers, amazed at the unflustered calm of the singers and bandsmen, were actually watching that recording, while the Red Arrows performed their aerial ballet live.

'It was brilliant!' says Chris Mann, who has always claimed that the RAF had got their sums wrong and had turned up one minute early.

'I finally had to tell him he was mad,' says Noel Vincent, the producer that day, who is now canon treasurer of Liverpool's Anglican cathedral. 'He could at least have told us that he had a Plan B.'

watter', a day's sail on the Caledonian McBrayne car-ferry *Jupiter*. The *Songs of Praise* mobile control van travelled on the car-deck, and hymns were performed on-board the ferry by travelling singers and a band, as well as ashore at Brodick in the Isle of Arran, Rothesay on Bute and Dunoon in the Cowal Peninsular. As we steamed into each bay, a different large crowd of singers was waiting hopefully, and in seconds Pam Rhodes, the presenter, and Ian McCrorie, the redoubtable conductor of Scotland's famous Toad Choir, had leapt ashore, followed by the cameras and sound crew.

*Right*: Series producer Roger Hutchings does the warm-up at RAF Scampton minutes before the early arrival of the Red Arrows in May 1993.

*Below*: Producer Chris Mann at RAF Scampton with his researcher Julia (now his wife).

## All aboard!

*Songs of Praise* is probably more suited to boats. Apart from the innumerable lifeboats that have been launched for our benefit, to the strains of 'Eternal Father, strong to save', several programmes have come from on-board larger vessels, including an aircraft carrier and the *QE2*. In Scotland, we managed a trip 'doon the

The most memorable moment for many people involving a ship was during the final hymn sung on *Songs of Praise* from the Falkland Islands. *Songs of Praise* was the first non-news programme to go there after the war. Just weeks after the liberation of the islands, Jim Murray, the then editor, and producer David Kremer flew out to Port Stanley where they recorded most of the programme on two film cameras in the tiny cathedral. For the final hymn, everyone stood on the deck of the *Rangotira*, one of the accommodation ships moored in the harbour, to sing 'Eternal Father, strong to save'. The final shot, filmed from a helicopter, zoomed back from the singers and the band of the First Hampshire Regiment to show the bleak, rural landscape that had so recently been the scene of conflict and where so many had lost their lives.

## Light of lights

It was Chris Mann, naturally, who uttered the words that best describe all the *Songs of Praise* derring-do events I've described in this chapter. 'Now you'll only get this once,' said Chris, as he prepared for *Songs of Praise*'s most brilliant and deafening pyrotechnics. *Songs of Praise* from Lewes in Sussex had set out to bring the light of Christ to the town in the season of the famous 5 November bonfire processions, with their distinctly un-ecumenical tradition and message.

'We shall retake the streets of Lewes for Christ,' was Chris's declared aim, so it was to end with God's own fireworks display, as the choirs, assembled under Lewes's old castle, broke into the chorus of 'Joy to the world!'. Chris teamed up with fireworks expert Phil 'the Jerb'. (The jerb is apparently one of his favourite firework-launching devices.) But Roger Hutchings had given Chris a strict limit to his fireworks budget, and even this was cut back and back as money was spent on other essentials for the programme. Finally Phil

said to Chris that he would provide a display worthy of 'Joy to the world!' by digging into his own pockets to make up the difference.

'Now, this is it,' said Chris, turning to Fiona Breslin, his assistant, as Roger Durston conducted the choirs in the gentle prayer of 'Glory to Thee, my God, this night', which was to come to an end just before the final chorus. 'Now! Cue the jerbs!'

'Fire mortar one! And two!' called Fiona, who was linked up to Phil.

'Listen, you can actually hear the whoosh!' enthused Chris, showing me a recording. 'The

Chris Mann (left) watches Phil 'the Jerb' preparing fireworks at Lewes Castle.

next moment, the control van was shaken by what seemed like an earth tremor on the word "Joy". Fiona's cueing was perfect. Half the choir screamed, but thank goodness, the other half kept singing.'

'Fire three! And four!' screamed Fiona.

'We were all rolling all over the place in the van,' said Chris, 'but Phil had done us proud. And can there ever have been a more brilliant image of what *Songs of Praise* is all about?'

# Calling the Tune

## The Music Makers of *Songs of Praise*

If you are travelling by train somewhere in Britain and the person opposite you is listening intently on his mobile phone to a caller who sounds as if they are singing a hymn, the chances are you are sharing a carriage with Robert Prizeman. As music advisor to *Songs of Praise*, this is the man who checks every suggestion and helps find the musicians and arrangements that will give each programme that vital mix of old favourites and surprising, new, fresh sounds. A human musical encyclopedia, relied on by every member of the BBC production team, it will not be surprising if Robert is looking a little harassed on your journey. It could be a summer day, but the anxious producer may need instant approval for a suggestion for the autumn harvest programme. Can Robert help find a brass quintet? And an arranger? By tomorrow, please?

Robert is a 'can-do' person; a musician who understands what it is like to train a choir to sing on TV and is certain that the congregation 'can do' too. For the singers

gathered to make *Songs of Praise*, he is the person on the end of yet another telephone, the one who is at the conductor's side during the recording. The uncanny experience of hearing a telephone suddenly ring in a Jacobean pulpit in a medieval church can be the source of much hilarity. After each hymn is recorded, the sound of the telephone ringing breaks the tense silence that usually follows what everyone hopes and believes is their best and final performance. But Robert is quite likely to come up with the astonishing proposal that they can have just one more 'go' and the sound will be twice as good.

*Songs of Praise*'s music advisor is not a sadist, but he is in a unique position to judge how good the sound will be. As each hymn or song is recorded, he is the first person to hear the performance through a loudspeaker in the control van, just as the audience will be hearing it on transmission. He isn't distracted by the atmosphere in the church; this makes the sound thrilling, but some of that magic quality can be lost on transmission. He is not only on the audience's side, but he is also the person who usually comes up with some simple suggestion that makes the singing easier. So you might say he is on the side of the angels.

Apart from his mobile phone occasionally bringing squeaky sounds from the BBC *Songs of Praise* hymn book to the railway carriage, Robert usually tries to remain incognito. He knows that the choice of hymn tunes is something people feel deeply about and can be the source of great dissension. Everyone knows the 'correct' tune for their own particular favourite words and they also know the mournful old tune or the ghastly modern one that should not be sung on their *Songs of Praise*. It is as well that the face of the person who makes the final decision remains unknown.

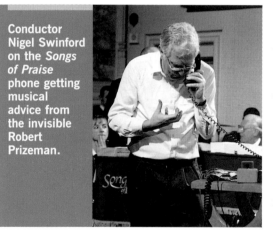

Conductor Nigel Swinford on the *Songs of Praise* phone getting musical advice from the invisible Robert Prizeman.

Owning up to choosing the hymn tunes myself in the past when editor, before the days of Robert, I had the chance to display my own musical prejudices, and soon discovered how rarely they were shared. One viewer wrote with the sinister warning that if in future I did not use the 'correct' tune for their own favourite hymn, then they would come and bang and rattle and beat on the church doors loudly until the singers obeyed. My memory tells me that they did not make it entirely clear what the 'correct' tune was, which is not unusual.

Sometimes the distinction can be quite small to the casual ear. Witness the difference between the tunes 'Moredun' and 'Was lebet' for 'O worship the Lord in the beauty of holiness'. In Scotland, for nearly everyone, 'Moredun' is the 'correct' tune. A few years ago, I found myself making a public apology in a church, bowing to demands to keep the choir on at the TV recording as we hastily switched to 'Moredun'. Then, later that same year, a couple of hundred miles north in Orkney, we remembered to bring 'Moredun' but everyone wanted 'Was lebet'. Percy Dearmer in *Songs of Praise Discussed* is no help, mentioning neither, and suggesting J.S. Bach's 'Crasselius' and Geoffrey Shaw's 'Dymchurch' instead.

**Personal choice**

Percy Dearmer's *Songs of Praise Discussed*, a handbook to the best-known hymns and the companion volume to Ralph Vaughan-Williams's *Songs of Praise* was, long ago before TV, my very first music advisor. I confess that the music for my very first *Songs of Praise* production 30 years ago was decided by using a far simpler, if more autocratic, method than the current democratic one of brainstorming by some of Britain's best choral musicians. One afternoon, my lifelong friend Christopher

Wroughton – who had sung as a boy treble in the Westminster Abbey Special Choir under Sir William McKie in the 1950s – and I shut ourselves in my parents' dining room. We had gathered together a pile of hymn books from all over the place so that we could work our way through an enormous list of suggestions supplied by the Council of Churches in Carlisle. Christopher strode up and down in the resonant space of the wooden-floored dining room, singing through all the hymns one by one, realizing as he went on that since his voice had broken he had rather lost his grip. Meanwhile I was trying to decide which hymn-book tempo was absolutely right for the acoustics of Carlisle's Methodist Central Hall, where the programme was to be recorded. We did not emerge from the dining room for a very late tea until we had reached our verdict. By the grace of God, the choirs survived our choice of words and music, which included some of Wesley's longest and most demanding hymns, but I never let my enthusiasm lead me into being quite so autocratic again.

In Scotland in the early days, Ronnie Falconer's method was to send out a form requesting the host church to submit a list of proposed hymns and tunes. The opening hymn was always already filled in: 'Ye Gates, lift up your heads' to the tune 'St George's, Edinburgh'. Robert Goodwin, now 81 years old, has been organist at Cartsburn-Augustine Church in Greenock for 50 years. He was at the console of the church's 1932 Brooks of Glasgow two-manual organ one night in 1961, for one of the earliest *Songs of Praise* recordings. The organ was 'all over the place and cyphering without warning', he remembers, 'sounding just like the *Queen Mary* going up the Clyde in a fog!' Somehow the engineers 'helped it to come out right'.

Good neighbourliness as Northern Ireland's Michael McCracken crosses the water to Kintyre in Scotland and conducts *Songs of Praise* from Campbeltown.

How this was done with the unsophisticated recording techniques of 1961 is a mystery; it may be that, like so many musicians, Mr Goodwin is his own sternest critic.

Brian Hardy's experience of selecting the music and conducting a *Songs of Praise* later in the 1960s reveals that innovation and experiment were welcome even then. In 1966 Brian, an Episcopalian priest, was jointly inducted with a Church of Scotland minister into the ecumenical parish of Livingston New Town. It was the first experiment of its kind in Scotland. People still had to be found to come and live in the new town before a joint congregation could be formed, so it was to be quite a challenge, a year or two later, when Livingston New Town was chosen as a venue for *Songs of Praise*.

'Ronnie Falconer was asking a lot from us,' says Brian, remembering the early days when the joint congregation met for worship in the town's first primary school, 'but he gave us freedom to experiment, especially with the music. We were also in a unique position as we did not have to unite for *Songs of Praise* – as we already were united!'

With only a piano for accompaniment, Brian was to conduct – but instead of making life easy for himself, he decided to push the boat out. He chose many new hymns to reflect the new situation. For the choir, drawn from among the local coal-miners and the Woman's Guild, he chose two very demanding special items. There was a modern setting by John Joubert of John Bunyan's hymn, 'He that is down needs fear no fall'; and then the tour de force, John Mason's text, 'Thou wast, O God', sung to the music from Ralph Vaughan-Williams's 'Fantasia on a theme of Thomas Tallis'. It all had to be rehearsed and recorded in one Sunday afternoon.

Unlike the sophisticated support offered today by Robert Prizeman and a team of professional music arrangers, Brian was his own arranger and typist too, preparing copies of the songs using a portable typewriter and an elderly duplicator kept for the weekly parish news.

'Actually, we were all thrilled while we were recording,' says Brian. 'The sound seemed so strong and full. I particularly remember the marvellous sight of my colleague, the Roman Catholic priest in Livingston, lustily singing Luther's hymn "Ein feste Burg". It made me realize that we were doing something worthwhile for the viewers. But, although doing *Songs of Praise* was a great encouragement for us, we were disappointed in the TV sound which lacked resonance and sounded thin.'

He says he envies today's conductors and their pulpit telephone calls from Robert Prizeman.

Today, wherever it comes from, *Songs of Praise* is not conducted by the local organist or music director, but by a small regular team of experienced musicians who are accustomed to the unusual demands of making music for a television programme. It seems improbable that Sir Malcolm Sargent or Sir Edward Elgar would have been prepared to accept telephone calls on the conductor's rostrum during their choir rehearsal.

Today's *Songs of Praise* conductors must combine the qualities of an Olympic athlete, psychotherapist and revivalist preacher all in the one evening. They must be the best of teachers, helping people learn to sing without admitting they need to. Andrew Maries begins his rehearsals with deep-breathing exercises for everyone (even the producer has felt the benefit). After a long day at work, voices have often 'rusted up' by the evening. Andrew's exercises usually generate much merriment as everyone makes peculiar loosening-up noises, and this laughter helps choirs who, coming from different churches, may be strangers to each other to get to know each other before the real work begins.

Geoff Ellerby's association with *Songs of Praise* goes back to his teenage days in Boston in Lincolnshire. Little did we know then, when he played in a youth group in a programme I made there in 1977, that 20 years later he would be working for me again, coaxing sweet sounds from a large choir and band in Scotland. On this occasion it was the time of the British Open, and the singers were perched on a grandstand overlooking the 18th tee of that great golf course, the Royal and Ancient at St Andrews, for a *Songs of Praise* which featured Christians from among the world's star golfers.

It was Geoff who ran the gauntlet of custard pies and buckets of water as he strove to maintain musical order in a special programme marking the annual clowns' service in Dalston, which remembers the great Grimaldi.

Paul Leddington-Wright must be a candidate for *The Guinness Book of Records*, having conducted a 60,000-strong congregation for *Songs of Praise*'s first programme in the year 2000, which came from Cardiff's Millennium Stadium. He is equally at home directing small groups, such as Coventry Cathedral's Chapter House Choir, the St Michael's Singers in Jerusalem, or his own band of singers in a recent, very moving programme for Holocaust Sunday. For Paul, the rapport with the singers and building relationships with people he has only just met give him immense enjoyment. As for the mega events – Paul also conducted Mersey Glory from Goodison Park, another blockbuster programme – 'They just sort of happen,' he says. 'You try not to remember that you are looking after 62,000 people. You have got to be a really good technician, musician and theologian if people are to have a good time. We are trying to create together an experience of worship which stands a chance of reaching viewers through the TV screen.'

'Teach me to dance to the beat of your heart, to move in the power of your Holy Spirit,' sang 2,500 Christians, a sea of upturned faces and swaying bodies, crammed into what Pam Rhodes called 'one of the most exciting and most familiar buildings in the world'. It was the first of two special programmes from the Sydney Opera House to mark the 2000 Olympic Games and there, in the heart of this most dramatic of places to make music, was Noel Tredinnick, one of *Songs of Praise*'s most familiar faces, in his equally familiar white tuxedo, complete with a bright-red

Noel Tredinnick in rehearsal.

carnation. 'One of our favourite conductors', said Pam as Noel put the Opera Australia Orchestra through its paces.

Noel has made All Souls', Langham Place, in London a household name for Christian musicians around the world, and demonstrates through the hugely successful 'Prom Praise' that popular orchestral music also has a place in celebrating faith. A regular church organist since the age of 13, Noel now conducts the 60-strong All Souls' Orchestra for worship every week. On the first Sunday in 2001 his orchestra began *Songs of Praise* with the opening bars of Strauss's 'Also Sprach Zarathustra', popularly known as

the theme music for Stanley Kubrick's film *2001: A Space Odyssey*. The music linked seamlessly into the opening words of the carol 'It came upon the midnight clear'. Noel particularly enjoys encouraging everyone to relax and sing, however inadequate they feel. I am myself living proof that it works.

Gordon Stewart is one of the newer members of the team, and he is the mystery star of the new *Songs of Praise* titles, in which, as if by magic, the conductor materializes in front of choirs, bands and singers in towns and villages everywhere. You will need to take part in *Songs of Praise* yourself to see him from the front.

**Making Music Live!**
In spite of all this talent and increasingly sophisticated recording equipment, even the most exotic digital enhancements cannot always help in some of the more demanding situations for *Songs of Praise*. How does the conductor ensure CD-quality stereo sound in the open air? Now add on a busy city centre and some noisy football supporters and see what results.

It was 80 years after Glasgow's George Square filled with charging police horses and angry strikers intent on a Soviet-style revolution, meaning the Riot Act had to be read, when conductor Jim Hunter and his huge *Songs of Praise* choir occupied the public square for a peaceable but no less noisy gathering. The BBC's Music Live

# O Praise Ye The Lord

TUNE : LAUDATE DONINUM

FROM THE ANTHEM 'HEAR MY WORDS, YE PEOPLE'
BY C HUBERT H PARRY (1848-1918)

Verse 1 - Unis

erse 2 - Ha

YE THE LORD

...ise ye the Lord!
...e him in the height;
...ce in his word,
...ngels of light;
...eavens adore him
...vhom ye were made,
...worship before him,
...rightness arrayed.

...raise ye the Lord!
...se him upon earth,
...uneful accord,
...sons of new birth;
...ise him who has
...s grace from abo...
...aise him who ha...
...o sing of his lov...

...praise ye the L...
...ll things that g...
...ach jubilant c...
...e-echo arou...
...oud organs,...
...orth tell in...
...nd sweet harp, th...
...Of what he has done.

O praise ye the Lord!
Thanksgiving and song
To him be outpoured
All ages along:
For love in creation,
For heaven restored,
For grace of salvation,
O praise ye the Lord!

WORDS : H W BAKER (...

events were centred on Glasgow for a whole weekend, bringing hundreds of musicians out onto the streets – everything from string quartets to a Radio 1 roadshow.

For Jim, there was only one short window of opportunity to record *Songs of Praise*, which in the tradition of Music Live had to be staged in an open space so that anyone who wanted to could come along and sing. All morning and all evening on the Saturday other events were happening in the huge square. But if the weather was kind and the choirs who were coming from all over the west of Scotland were in good voice, then a couple of hours would just suffice for the BBC cameras dotted all around the square to record a happy event...

It is beginning to look like rain. Jim is no pessimist, but he does hold the record for conducting the wettest open-air *Songs of Praise* of all time. That too was in Glasgow and, as the Music Live rehearsal begins, the

sky is grey and threatening. It feels more like winter than midsummer as Jim, dressed in a white dinner jacket, leaps around the front of a huge platform on which some of Scotland's best musicians are assembled. Some of the music parts have vanished. 'They were on that chair,' says Jim, pointing to a space where no chairs now exist. The stewards have hijacked them for the growing choir and so, not for the first time, outward serenity on the faces of the production team disguises internal panic. The parts are found, but now some of the musicians have vanished. 'We'll just have to press on,' says Jim, speaking on a public-address system which is audible all over the city centre.

'Now, who doesn't know the first hymn?'

Hands go up. 'OK,' he says, 'welcome to a wonderful tune. Thirty seconds now to look at the notes and then we'll see how we do.'

A few seconds later Jim, exuding confidence with a dazzling smile, combined with a comedian's skill of suddenly turning his head to catch the attention of the now vast choir surrounding him on three sides, calls, 'Right. Now we know the notes, all ready, one – two and…!' He knows that they won't let him down.

The orchestra produces a huge sound, engulfing passing shoppers with the opening

**Noel Tredinnick conducting Christmas *Songs of Praise* from Trafalgar Square.**

bars introducing the hymn tune 'St Denio'. It is dramatic, it is uplifting – but it is completely unrecognizable until the familiar hymn tune gradually takes over, gently accompanying the singers for the first verse of 'Immortal, invisible, God only wise'. Singers who have been conducted by Jim Hunter before know better than to come along unprepared for music arrangements full of surprises, blending strings with electric guitars, trombones and timpani with drumkits. Anything may happen musically, especially in Jim's interpretations of his colleague Dave Pringle's reworkings of familiar hymns, which, while not always scoring highly with some purists, are a sell-out in high-street record stores.

'Has anyone seen the helicopter?' calls Jim after the hymn ends. 'Next time we will film this hymn and… no, don't look up. The helicopter should fly over us, filming us while you are singing. You can be twice as superb. Yes you can! It's our one chance of getting a helicopter shot for *Songs of Praise* showing the city at its best.'

The crowd laughs and choristers zip up anoraks to their necks. Glasgow is feeling far from its best – cold, with grey clouds and spots of rain in the air. Even Diane-Louise Jordan cannot persuade her co-presenter, TV's popular weatherman Ian Macaskill, to forecast a silver lining for them. In fact, the passing helicopter is Jim Hunter's ingenious way of making the best of a bad job. For this very afternoon the Scottish cup final is being played barely a mile away. So the weather is not the only hazard because, regardless of the result, boisterous supporters singing distinctly un-hymn-like songs will be filtering back through George Square later in the day. Jim, who uniquely in *Songs of Praise* combines the two roles of conductor and BBC producer, has persuaded the TV director of the cup-final coverage to divert the football 'eye-in-the-sky' over George Square en route to the big match. So this will be a silver lining of sorts.

Suddenly the helicopter appears through the darkening sky and Jim declares full-speed ahead. There are moments in the performance when, knees bent, he almost seems to launch himself at the singers; then, straightening up like a giant to mark out the more majestic moments in a familiar hymn, he demonstrates a display of energy with which I have so often seen him transform mundane singing into an exciting expression of faith.

Around 5 p.m. the match is over. 'Celtic 1, Rangers 0,' says Jim

to the choir without a trace of the partisan in his voice or demeanour, 'but you're going to make this last hymn the praise of God which unites this whole city.'

'Now. Where are the pipers?' he calls out to me, looking around the fringe of the crowd into which the odd benign but noisy football supporter is beginning to filter. The police also advise that they will have to let traffic back into the road around the square in 20 minutes.

'Quick! Go and find the pipers,' Jim says to me. Even though I am, at least in theory, in charge, these pipers are news to me, but having a job to do is perhaps the best way of coping with stress. How I found the City of Glasgow Pipe Band hidden away down a side-street and how they followed me, marching in quick time to the square just in time to play in the last verse of 'Stand up, stand up for Jesus', will have to be a story for another book.

N i n e

# One of the Family

### Presenting *Songs of Praise*

It was going to be the perfect eye-catching beginning to *Songs of Praise* for Advent Sunday. A huge choir was ready to sing 'Our God reigns' in the People's Palace, the elegant Victorian glass building on Glasgow Green. Lit up on this particular December night in 1992, it looked magical from outside.

The idea was that Pam Rhodes should arrive outside the palace by horse and cart. No ordinary horse, but a huge, beautifully groomed Clydesdale, the sort that once was used to deliver provisions around the city. A camera on a high crane would record just the scene needed to encourage channel-hopping viewers to stay with *Songs of Praise*.

The only problem was, as you may remember from an earlier chapter, that instead of 'Our God reigns', it was 'Our God rains'. A fine drizzle had turned into a downpour and although it was still light and warm in the People's Palace, it was so dark outside that Pam, who had arrived with the cheerful enthusiasm so familiar to TV viewers, could not even see the waiting horse and cart.

'Are you serious?' she asked me as we all paddled through Glasgow's answer to a monsoon, everyone trying to protect Pam's hair with a forest of umbrellas. 'Where's the camera that I'm speaking to?' she asked.

'Don't look until we're ready to record,' I said, 'but it's up there.' I pointed through the umbrellas to the moonless heavens and only the distant, friendly 'hello' of the camera operator gave Pam any clue where it was.

Pam gave me a look of grim determination, leapt onto the cart and rapidly set about making friends with the young but very damp singers who had vied for a place alongside the 'woman from the telly'.

'We could be out here for hours,' muttered one of the team. 'She has only had a minute to learn a one-minute link.'

They had seriously underestimated our most experienced presenter. Pam Rhodes is the brilliant one-take perfectionist of *Songs of Praise*.

## True professionals

There is probably only one time in the week when Pam Rhodes won't answer the telephone, which seems to ring constantly when she is at home in Hertfordshire. As *Songs of Praise* begins, her cats Pickle, Sassy and Lily, together with Dylan the Villain, the dieting Labrador, settle down with her for 35 minutes of concentrated viewing.

'No, the rest of the family don't usually join me,' she says with a rueful smile, 'but I know my mum will be watching and we will be on the phone to each other as soon as it's over. She can be quite critical, especially if I've presented the programme.'

'Welcome to the youth club,' is Pam's greeting when I call to see her, as an explanation of all the hectic activity going on around the family home. The door is opened by Bethan, one of her two children. Bethan and brother Max are growing up fast and are quite keen that their friends popping in and out of the house do not hear about their vignette roles on past *Songs of Praise* programmes.

'They both came on the programme I made in Benidorm, and on *Songs of Praise* from York Max was filmed with me on an Easter-egg hunt, which is something we always do every year at home,' Pam explained.

'Mum, why didn't you tell me what a prat I looked!' Max had observed when he saw the programme.

'I think if I had gone on to present *Come Dancing* that really would have been the end.'

Pam is a person of many talents, a singer and dancer as well as an author and presenter. And, if popularity is measured by the number of telephone conversations she has when *Songs of Praise* is not on, then she must be the nation's favourite. While many presenters will have kept in touch with people they have met on the programme, Pam actually keeps a little book at her side of everyone that she has ever met on *Songs of Praise*. This extended family

Pam Rhodes with 'the team' filming on the 18th green at St Andrew's.

rings her with news of triumphs and woes. Between calls, Pam says, 'It's because I know how much courage it takes even just to say "hello" on TV.'

Many people have now shared their stories in their first, and perhaps only, appearance in front of the camera. After the cameras have gone, people are left with all the difficulties and all the questions that can come up in speaking with honesty about their faith.

'For me, after 26 years of presenting TV, it's not a taxing job, but it's very, very hard for them, and of course they give me back so much personal support too,' Pam describes.

Pam's first *Songs of Praise* came from nearby St Albans on Easter Sunday. She did feel very nervous then, especially as she was being filmed walking at the head of a procession of pilgrims right across Hertfordshire to the cathedral. 'The people just behind me were really friendly and helped me through.'

As Pam later discovered, they were not only friends from *Songs of Praise*: 'It was the

Geoffrey Wheeler introduces the 25th-anniversary *Songs of Praise* from Wesley's Chapel, London, in 1983.

first week after I had moved house, and I went for the first time to the church I now attend, where I found everyone very welcoming. Later, when I was watching a recording of the pilgrimage to St Albans, I recognized that the people walking behind me, who had helped me through my first *Songs of Praise* piece to camera, were the very same people who had now made me welcome into the family of my new church –

a church that I had just happened to pick out of the blue.'

With almost 200 presenters – who at different times have all become 'one of the family' to regular viewers – introducing more than 1,700 editions of *Songs of Praise* between them, mentioning everyone who richly deserves their place in the story of 'the nation's favourite' is impossible. But one person who became 'Mr *Songs of Praise*' over the first half of its 40-year history is Geoffrey Wheeler. Being the firm but friendly quizmaster of TV's *Top of the Form* meant that Geoffrey would always be mobbed at the end of *Songs of Praise* by young (and not-so-young) autograph hunters. Older people sought his signature (always written painstakingly in what looked like Sanskrit) because they liked his gently voiced introductions, which owed much to his other life as a Church of England layreader.

Geoffrey was the easiest of colleagues for any nervous young producer and he had an impish sense of humour which would emerge to help everyone relax in troubled times. He was usually responsible for an awful pun or two in the tense moments before *Songs of Praise* began. Once, he was completely outdone with a truly dreadful Shakespearean example from the late Bishop Stewart Cross, who was directing the programme in the Lancashire town of Bury and was completing a microphone check with his presenter just as the church clock struck six o'clock. 'Friends, Romans and countrymen,' repeated Geoffrey, who knew a good one when he heard it. 'I come to Bury six heures – not to praise hymn!' The congregation groaned.

Geoffrey Wheeler bore *Songs of Praise*'s first great test of trying to match the mood of the nation on a sad day. By the end of January 1965, it was clear that Sir Winston Churchill was close to death. *Songs of Praise* was planned to come from Harrow School, which Sir Winston had attended. Of course no one knew exactly when the great man would die, nor could they write the script in advance. Would there be time to record the programme, or would it have to come live from the school? Geoffrey remembers the moment in his *Sunday Morning Record Show*, on the *Light Programme* on 24 January, when the producer warned him over his headphones, 'Don't speak at the end of this record.' When it ended, a sombre announcer took over to announce the death of Sir Winston.

'We just had enough time to mount a "live" *Songs of Praise*,' Geoffrey describes. He remembers travelling out on the Metropolitan line to Harrow-on-the-Hill and walking up to the school, thinking all the while of what words would be appropriate for the programme that evening. Colin James, a BBC producer and later bishop of Winchester (now retired) was waiting with Derek Burrell-Davis, one of the BBC's legendary directors of TV outside broadcasts:

'It was very emotionally involving for me, with 300 boys singing, and I remember an extraordinary shot of a bust of Sir Winston in the foreground while the choir sang in the

Roger Royle introduces *Songs of Praise* from Eastbourne promenade in summer 1985.

background. It was very unusual then to do the programme live, and I found that I had to keep thinking of something down-to-earth as I spoke to the camera at such an emotional gathering, so that I wouldn't let the side down.' *Songs of Praise* live at 6.50 p.m. that evening was seen by an audience exceeding 10 million. It was a record not broken until a programme from Scotland 25 years later during the Gulf War. Writing afterwards to the BBC, the headmaster of Harrow School, Dr Robert James, praised the 'wonderful piece of education for the whole school' which was seeing Geoffrey and the BBC team at work so superbly and under such difficult circumstances.

I have many personal memories of other presenters who have sometimes transformed my own scripts into powerful television moments: Tom Fleming, telling the story of the carpenter from Nazareth in an old woodworking shop in Amersham; Leonard Pearcy, picking up all the nuances of Christmas in the Suffolk village of Clare in a specially filmed *Songs of Praise* with the composer John Rutter and Clare College choir; and Roger Royle, the priest and presenter who is now the voice of Radio 2's *Sunday Half-Hour*, who is for me God's own comedian. How Roger converted my own intricately written history of the Battle of Hastings into fewer than 20 hilarious seconds as he introduced *Songs of Praise* from Eastbourne is still a personal source of wonder.

In recent years, and before his *Ground Force* success, Alan Titchmarsh travelled across Britain in a *Songs of Praise* series, which took him eventually to the cradle of Celtic Christianity, Iona. It was high summer and the sun had still not set at 10.30 in the evening when Alan arrived and was asked to muse aloud standing on a rock, with the rising tide far out in the Sound of Iona.

Alan had begun a very long day at the wheel of the Morgan sportscar that Simon Hammond, the producer, hoped might attract new viewers to *Songs of Praise* (car enthusiasts, presumably). Alan had to drive

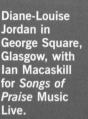
Diane-Louise Jordan in George Square, Glasgow, with Ian Macaskill for *Songs of Praise* Music Live.

in a thoroughly safety-conscious way across the narrow roads of the West Highlands of Scotland while being filmed by two cameras mounted on the car. Any other presenter might have been expected to be soundly asleep by sundown, but, as the tide rose higher and higher and night fell, Alan kept going to the last minute. 'I'll just do one more "muse" for you, but if you want any more you'll have to bring me a snorkel.'

Hazardous filming is a run-of-the-mill activity for Diane-Louise Jordan after her success presenting *Blue Peter*. Diane-Louise absolutely bursts with energy and she holds a strange *Songs of Praise* record for surviving more than three-quarters of an hour of non-stop jiving for the camera on a weekday morning. Producer Justin Adams, making a programme to commemorate the work of the

Lifeboat Service from Tynemouth, had engaged 'Doc' Cox, of *That's Life!* fame, to perform a very perky song about caring. 'Doc' and Justin persuaded Diane-Louise and their pensioner host at the Lifeboat Museum in Tynemouth to interpret the song by dancing

*Above*: Sally Magnusson, floor manager Brian MacBeath and make-up supervisor Michelle Coletta between hymns at Glamis Castle.

*Right*: Alan Titchmarsh on the road with film recordist Arthur Chesterman in summer 1991.

on camera as it was sung. I am glad this spontaneous sequence was included in the final programme, as the performers made it both humorous and moving. No serious *Songs of Praise* editor in their right mind would have approved such an idea in advance. For me, *Songs of Praise* has always been all the better when showing that religious broadcasting can be entertaining.

A newcomer to the programme, but one who is going straight to people's hearts, is Aled Jones, walking on the ground these days, not in the air, now his famous treble voice has broken, but still sure to become 'one of the family'. It was with the words from *The Snowman*, which made him so famous, that

he introduced himself to a hard-pressed choir preparing for *Songs of Praise* from St Mary Redcliffe in Bristol. In an instant, with a gale of laughter and applause, the choir relaxed and found new energy.

Sally Magnusson, who presented *Songs of Praise* for many years far from her native Scotland, had to present the other face of the programme's role as 'one of the family' on Mothering Sunday in March 1996. The world's media had converged on the little town of Dunblane following the terrible attack on the primary school. Sally, a mother of five young children, had to find her own words after a day spent with the grief-stricken people of the town. Acutely concerned lest the BBC Scotland cameras intruded, she knew nevertheless that the audience would be looking to *Songs of Praise* that evening for insight and comfort. Never before had I seen a presenter working under such pressure.

For her main introduction to the programme, Sally sat surrounded by the mountains of flowers that lay all round Dunblane Cathedral, expressing the sympathy of a shocked world. Just yards away, people were praying in the tiny Clement Chapel as she spoke as quietly as was technically feasible:

'Today is Mothering Sunday, and there can't be a mother in the land who didn't receive her card, a flower, an embrace without aching for the mothers of Dunblane whose arms are empty. But it's not just mothers, it's fathers, it's everyone. If ever the people of a nation can be said to have shared each other's pain, felt it like a big knot in the pit of the stomach that won't go away, it's surely now. Today they came to their ancient cathedral to look for solace, and we've come to share that too.'

Pam Rhodes found herself faced with the same kind of challenge, having to present a *Songs of Praise* reflecting the mood of a grief-struck audience fewer than 24 hours after the death of Diana, Princess of Wales, in August 1997.

She had begun that Sunday on location in the Suffolk countryside, filming an interview for another *Songs of Praise*, when the then series producer, David Kremer, called her on her mobile phone. *Songs of Praise* would be live that night and she must get ready to present it. He did not even know where it would come from, but Helen Alexander, *Songs of Praise*'s editor at that time, was trying to get back from a conference in Geneva to be with her to discuss the script, and Stephen Benson would direct it.

Pam seems made for these sorts of moments. As she puts it, 'I find when times are really tough and I'm on live, a calm comes over me. To be professional working with a TV crew, you have to be absolutely predictable. And I always prepare a Plan B at the least. What I always remember, though, is that I am talking through the camera to one interested, friendly person watching *Songs of Praise*.'

In front of the huge congregation that had flooded into London's St Paul's Cathedral, which Pam described as 'the parish church of the nation', she spoke faultlessly to her 'one interested, friendly person'.

'We are together,' Pam said, 'to pray for those who grieve, to sing hymns which express the feelings it's hard for us to find the right words for, and to reach out to God at a time when we are reminded how precious and fragile is the gift of life.'

When, towards the end of that extraordinary, almost spontaneous programme, live pictures of the plane bringing the Princess's body back to Northolt were shown while the choir was singing, viewers were witness to an unprecedented collaboration between the BBC newsroom and the religious broadcasting teams. Never before had the two worlds come together like this. The image of a small jet plane landing in the evening light to be met by a sad and sombre party gave a deeper meaning to the words of a psalm and a hymn being sung at the same moment in the cathedral.

Pam told me recently, 'We hadn't even been sure that there would be anyone there, but it was when the live broadcast had ended that the most astonishing thing happened. As the congregation went out, another equally huge congregation came in to sit in silence in the nave.'

*Songs of Praise*'s ability to respond to these sad events, as with other editions put together at short notice – for example during the 1991 Gulf War and following the tragic deaths of the children and their teacher at Dunblane Primary School – is one of the reasons why, as the programme reaches its 40th anniversary, it is trusted like a family friend and still commands a big, loyal audience.

Just as the equipment was being cleared away, the full impact of all that had happened that day hit Pam. Someone with a small but beautiful voice had found a microphone that was still live. Entirely without accompaniment and with sweetness and simplicity in the middle of the silent crowds she sang 'Be still for the presence of the Lord':

*Be still, for the presence of the Lord,*
 *the Holy One is here;*
*Come, bow before Him now,*
 *with reverence and fear.*
*In Him no sin is found,*
 *we stand on holy ground.*
*Be still, for the presence of the Lord,*
 *the Holy One is here…*

*Be still, for the power of the Lord*
 *is moving in this place,*
*He comes to cleanse and heal,*
 *to minister His grace.*
*No work too hard for Him,*
 *in faith receive from Him;*
*Be still, for the power of the Lord*
 *is moving in this place.*

Dave Evans

# Harry and Thora

## A Tribute to Two Great Stars

'An entertainer leaves a little of himself behind after he has gone.' So wrote Sir Harry Secombe, one of Britain's funniest and best of men, in the preface to his autobiography, *Arias and Raspberries*. But I am certain that, like me, his theatre, film, television and radio audiences, who are numbered in millions, who loved him, admired him and laughed with him for almost 80 years, would want just for once to disagree. Through song, laughter and tears, Harry's goodness touched many lives and perhaps never more so than in his Sunday-evening appearances on *Songs of Praise* and *Highway*.

So I prefer another of Harry's regular quips when he was making those programmes, both on and off the camera: 'Goon, but not forgotten!'

And that is how a special *Songs of Praise* tribute to him in autumn 2000 began with a song and ended with a raspberry.

As Harry, following a long struggle with ill-health after a stroke, came onto the stage of Guildford's Yvonne Arnand Theatre, he certainly wasn't receiving the first standing ovation of his life, but it was one of the most heartfelt. This was an occasion when the *Songs of Praise* audience, every seat in the house packed, was happy to turn itself into a choir to make a special programme as a tribute to someone they really loved. After an hour's strenuous hymn practice with conductor Noel Tredinnick, everyone was being rewarded with their first glimpse of one of TV's most familiar faces.

### The rivals

For Harry, it had begun in 1981 when the opera-singer and star of stage, screen and *The Goon Show* was launched as ITV's new secret weapon in the ratings battle with *Songs of Praise*. For 10 years, Sir Harry was the face of *Highway*. For six weeks of each year he found himself competing for an audience against an old friend, the star of the BBC's *Praise Be!*, Dame Thora Hird. Personally, it was the friendliest of competitions, although whenever a helicopter puttered overhead while Harry was on location with *Highway*, he always assured his interviewees that it was Thora's helicopter intent on mischief. By the time *Highway* came to an end, Thora had been a guest on the show but, much to everybody's regret, Harry never made it onto *Praise Be!*

However, with the end of ITV's early-Sunday-evening religious programmes in 1991 Helen Alexander realized that it was the moment to try to persuade Sir Harry to join her *Songs of Praise* team, and come to work for his old rival. It was to be a happy and successful transfer. Back on the road, Harry was insistent that he must not upstage the people he saw as the real stars of *Songs of Praise* – the talented singers and musicians in the local communities and, most particularly, the people who tell their stories every week. Although he had been a choirboy in his local church in Swansea and his brother Fred became an Anglican priest, it was in his years of listening to people telling their stories of extraordinary courage and hope that Sir Harry felt he really experienced faith at work. 'I've learned more to lean on God,' he mused.

A few years before, while filming *Songs of Praise* for Remembrance Sunday, ex-Lance Bombardier Secombe 924387 joined 'Smiler', one of the now-vanished survivors of the First World War, in the war cemetery at Bethune. Carrying a wreath of poppies, he gently pushed Smiler, 101-year-old wheelchair-bound Albert

Marshall, around the graves as together they looked for the last resting place of Smiler's best mate. When they found it, they stood together in silence. Harry said later, 'You can't tell people what war is like. You just keep quiet, sharing memories with your comrades.' The scene showed Harry at his most sensitive, caring but unembarrassed by Smiler's tears.

I worked with Harry on *Highway* as well as on *Songs of Praise*, and never ceased to marvel at his capacity for being truly himself on-screen. Unusually for a famous celebrity, the

Below: Sir Harry tries out a birthday gift from the crew with Andrew Barr (as *Highway* producer), Sussex, 1989.

man you saw on the TV was the real Harry. He would not have known how to be a prima donna if he had tried and was, truly, exactly as nice as he seemed. He was also one of only a handful of comedians who, without a team of scriptwriters, was naturally extremely funny. Anyone who wants to prove the link between laughter and God could do no better than to remember the nation's favourite star, who made Neddy Seagoon, his character from *The Goon Show*, a household name.

It was natural for Harry that, when he fell

seriously ill while presenting *Songs of Praise*, he wanted no fuss and only felt that he should go on making the programme if he could give 100 per cent of his attention to the people he was meeting. Prostate cancer had been diagnosed and then Harry suffered a stroke. The future was bleak, but Harry wasn't defeated. Producers Siân Salt and Medwyn Hughes, a fellow Welshman, asked Harry if he would share his determination and journey of recovery with television viewers. What emerged from the filming, which followed Harry as he struggled to regain his power of

Sir Harry filming *Songs of Praise* in Blackpool with Ken Dodd, watched by producer Medwyn Hughes.

movement and his speech let alone his singing voice, was a tremendously moving documentary for the BBC's *Everyman*, watched by one of the largest audiences ever for that series.

Harry's almost wordless courage was complemented by the natural sense of humour and love of his wife Myra, which *Songs of Praise* viewers had previously seen when the couple had renewed their marriage vows on a Valentine's Day programme. Harry explained in his interview with Pam Rhodes, on the stage of the Yvonne Arnand Theatre, that not only was

it Myra's love and care, but also the stories of all the people he had met over the years on *Songs of Praise* and *Highway*, that had most helped him on his long road to recovery. He too had come to understand the calm and contentment that can be experienced even in dire circumstances.

Among many celebrities and people from all walks of life who came forward to pay tribute was Harry's godson, Alastair, and his mother, Wendy Craig. They performed a song that Wendy had written called 'Show me the way', which moved Harry very much. And then came the grand finale – the entire London Welsh Male Voice Choir in their smart red jackets with their conductor, Haydn James, pouring through every entrance into the auditorium and joining Harry and Pam on-stage. They sang a spectacular arrangement of 'Onward, Christian soldiers' to the great Welsh tune 'Rachie'. In that Guildford theatre it was the nearest *Songs of Praise* has ever come to evoking the spirit of a Victorian revivalist meeting.

The programme ended delightfully with the audience blowing a collective and deafening raspberry at the ex-Goon. He loved it.

### The first lady

Another version of 'Onward, Christian soldiers', sung, she would insist, to the 'correct' tune 'St Gertrude', is a favourite of Harry's sparring partner from the days of competition between *Praise Be!* and *Highway*, Dame Thora Hird.

Thora paid her own fond tribute to Sir Harry that night.

If anyone's name is synonymous with 'the nation's favourite', it must surely be Thora's; in her ninth decade she is still winning top international acting awards. I first met Dame Thora when she was starring in *The First Lady*, a series set in Bradford in which she played the mayor of a north-country town. My job as assistant sound recordist was to make sure that the microphone was in the right place to record her visiting the fictional corporation waterworks. That was harder than it sounds, because a huge thumping pump worked by a hissing steam engine dominated the scene and hearing the dialogue was almost impossible. Thora understood my problem perfectly and found her way to the microphone without fuss, but she never once stepped out of mayoral character in all the hours of filming. We all found ourselves treating her as though she really was the mayor. I could not believe that she hadn't actually been one at some time in her life.

When *Songs of Praise* began in 1961, Thora was starring in TV's *Meet the Wife* with Freddie Frinton playing her stage husband. My mother never missed an episode, and I only wish I could remember more about the scene where Thora and Freddie got into a terrible muddle with the vicar. I am sure Thora deployed her 'posh' voice, used sparingly but hilariously and

to such great effect in *In Loving Memory* and *Last of the Summer Wine*.

When I became editor of *Songs of Praise* more than 20 years ago, I suggested we should try Thora in her own series, reading viewers' letters and introducing their favourite hymns sung on past *Songs of Praise* programmes. Thora had already spoken about her own favourite hymn in a programme made by Ray Short, and there had been a regular summer series repeating what we thought were the best hymns from *Songs of Praise* with Barbara Mullen (the original Janet in *Dr Finlay's*

*Left*: Dame Thora visits Liz Barr at home in Scotland.

*Right*: Dame Thora helps Chris Mann find the best bluebells in Sussex for *Praise Be!*

*Casebook*). Now we would ask viewers to make their own choice.

They did so by the thousands. As we made the first series of programmes, it was amazing to see how Thora, a tiny figure sitting alone in a big television studio, seemed to look right through the camera into each viewer's home and chat as though she were a friendly visitor who had come to call. What is more, *Praise Be!* started to do what thousands of viewers had been requesting for years and years as Thora said, 'Let's have the hymn words on the screen for this one.'

Like Harry, she is an absolute natural on-screen and off. Thora and Liz (my wife), the scriptwriter, got on tremendously well. They both come from the north country and share the same mixture of direct talking, sharp wit and great kindness. From the professional relationship on TV and in the books they have written together has developed a great friendship.

Many people were surprised to hear that there was a script when Thora was on. They could not believe that it wasn't spontaneous as she opened letters and appeared to read them just a couple of minutes before the next hymn came on. It wasn't quite so simple. Every link had to be carefully timed, as all broadcasting has to be, with up to seven full-length programmes to be recorded in just two days. But however natural Thora appeared, she is an arch-professional, and she would always time her links to the split second.

*Praise the Lord*, with the presenter in close-up sitting in a studio in front of an inoffensive but neutral back wall, developed into the elaborate 'sitting-room' stage set of *Your Songs of Praise Choice*, with Thora on a sofa and almost hidden by tropical plants. Finally, with *Praise Be!*, Thora presented the programmes from her family home in Sussex.

Of course it wasn't the home that Thora shared with Freddie Frinton, but with her real and devoted husband, Scotty. Thora's daughter, the film actress Janette Scott, allowed the BBC to use a large drawing room in the family home across the garden from where Thora and Scotty had a country cottage. As time went by, the *Praise Be!* team spread itself, testing Jan's kindness and patience to the limit, filming Thora in every room in the house, and the programmes usually opened to find her walking about the grounds with a procession of ducks and dogs trailing along behind her.

Over the years Thora's relationship with the *Praise Be!/Songs of Praise* viewers just grew and grew. For the first years of our own married life, Liz and I became used to our own small cottage being turned into a cross between a postal sorting office and Father Christmas's den whenever preparations began for a new series of *Praise Be!* Each week, thousands of letters, far more than Thora could cope with on her own, came in from viewers. We used to sift through them. Some of them ran to pages and pages and in the end all had to be discussed with Thora. She always wanted to include everyone. 'But Thora, there won't be any time for the hymns,' Liz used to say in desperation. Thora could be resolute. 'I can say it in less than three seconds. This lady's daughter has had arthritis for 27 years and is going to have another operation. I know it'll make all the difference to her. I'll just give her a mention.'

It was the letters asking Thora to come to tea that really got to me. It was as if so many ill and lonely viewers thought all would be well if only Thora would call on them. She didn't have to bring the cameras, they said. Just seeing her would be enough, the person they felt they all knew and wanted to say 'thank you' to, for all the pleasure she was bringing by playing their favourite hymns with the 'correct' tune.

Although it was never possible to visit those viewers, Thora did include several teatime conversations in *Praise Be!* She called in to see Dr David Hope, who is now archbishop of York. Then he was bishop of London and Thora somehow managed to inspect his fine-bone-china teacups while the hospitable bachelor was boiling the kettle. It was the beginning of a warm friendship that still endures.

In the last few years, since the death of her beloved Scotty and in spite of an incredibly heavy schedule of work, Dame Thora has come to Scotland to visit us, while Liz helped her to write the second and third volumes of her autobiography. When it comes to being 'the nation's favourite', Thora is clearly a tremendous favourite of the people of Scotland. She always likes to join in with our everyday activities but a visit to the shops with her is a slow business – it always brings the crowds out.

Ever since our meeting on *The First Lady*, I have loved every moment spent in Thora's company. When Scotty was alive, I used to get out my collection of 78 r.p.m. records and a wind-up gramophone and test them both on their knowledge of the hits of long ago. 'Who's Been Polishing the Sun' and 'When You Played the Organ and I Sang the Rosary' were two that stumped most of our friends, but not Thora and Scotty. Now, whenever we speak on the telephone, she continues the custom begun around our dinner table of reciting one of those great music-hall monologues like Stanley Holloway's 'Albert and the Lion'. I don't get a hymn to wake me up in the morning when she's with us, but a verse or two of 'I've never seen a straight banana' has often announced that breakfast is ready.

Like Sir Harry, Dame Thora is truly what she seems, and, because of the part she played in *Praise Be!*, she was, like Sir Harry, the natural choice for a tribute programme with Pam Rhodes, which included Harry's own serenade, as she headed for her 90th year. If proof were needed, the huge audiences for both programmes showed that these two great stars would remain the all-time favourites of millions.

*When I'm confused Lord, show me the way.*
  *Show me,*
  *show me the way;*

*Baffled and bruised, Lord show me the way.*
  *Show me,*
  *show me the way.*

*Still my heart and clear my mind,*
  *prepare my soul to hear your still, small voice,*
  *your word of truth.*
*Peace be still! Your Lord is near;*
  *always so close to show you the way,*
  *show you,*
  *show you the way.*

Wendy Craig

## *Eleven*

# Forty Years On

## A Glimpse of the Future

Pitch dark. Day has yet to dawn in the Yorkshire Wolds. Bible-black, like Dylan Thomas's world of *Under Milk Wood*, and a time when only Captain Cat can be heard muttering in his dream-laden sleep. In such a cold and unpromising darkness, the monks of Ampleforth are singing their first songs of praise for the new day. Obedient to the Rule of St Benedict written almost 1,500 years ago, 30 men both young and old, their heads shrouded in dark cowls, have come silently into the dimly lit choir of the great Abbey Church of St Laurence to sing Matins. They begin precisely on the last stroke of the 6 a.m. bell.

Every day, in accordance with the Benedictine Rule, the monks gather seven times for worship. By the end of each week, they have sung every one of the 150 Psalms. St Benedict believed that this was God's work, singing these ancient Bible hymns, a way that the mind and heart of man could be brought to God. 'O my strength, it is you to whom I

turn; for you, O God, are my strength, the God who shows me love to meet the new day' (Psalm 58).

The monks of the Ampleforth Community assemble in a building which, in the dim pre-dawn light, seems ancient, but which was actually completed in October 1961 and so is exactly the same age as *Songs of Praise*. It had taken 30 years to build, and was designed by the famous Victorian architect Giles Gilbert Scott. His prescription for a new church was always that there was 'plenty of elbow room', which also means a good space for TV cameras. *Songs of Praise* has been broadcast twice from the great vaulted church with which it shares a birthday.

Like the Benedictine community, the future of *Songs of Praise*, and whether it will be of any help to future generations, will depend on whether it can keep up its ancient tradition of singing hymns in praise of God, and yet remain always open to change and new ideas.

## The next forty years

So is there a secure future for *Songs of Praise* as it begins its fifth decade? I asked Hugh Faupel, the current editor – who has the task of convincing succeeding BBC controllers that the programme deserves its placing at peak time on the BBC's most popular channel – how he sees the future of this veteran of the TV schedules:

*When you are given responsibility for the United Kingdom's longest-running religious programme, you discover two things very quickly. First – love it or loathe it – everybody has an opinion about* Songs of Praise *and will quickly tell you what it is. Secondly, you discover that, as the editor, it is impossible to please everybody all the time.*

Songs of Praise *is one of those programmes that engages with people's emotions. Viewers feel that* Songs of Praise *belongs to them. It's a programme that is bigger than any presenter, producer or editor, and will survive them all. For me, music is the key to* Songs of Praise's *continued success. When we asked viewers to nominate their favourite hymn, we were pleasantly surprised when thousands of viewers responded and came up with more than 400 nominations, such is the continuing appeal of hymnody.*

*As the editor, I am all too aware of the need to provide viewers with the very best inspirational music. There will always be a place for the traditional 'karaoke', 'singalong' hymn-singing, but* there is also a place for top-quality solo and choir performance items. The challenge for Songs of Praise is to remain true to its hymn-singing roots but to include the broad range of inspirational music that touches both the heart and the soul. We may not get it right all the time – but we'll certainly keep singing.

For the record, the current top-ten hymns are:

1. 'O Lord, my God, when I, in awesome wonder' ('How Great Thou Art')

2. 'Dear Lord and Father of mankind'

3. 'The day thou gavest, Lord, is ended'

4. 'Great is thy faithfulness'

5. 'Be still, for the presence of the Lord'

6. 'What a friend we have in Jesus'

7. 'Make me a channel of your peace'

8. 'Love Divine, all loves excelling'

9. 'O Love that wilt not let me go'

10. 'On a hill far away' ('The Old Rugged Cross')

Paul Leddington-Wright, conductor of the great *Songs of Praise* 40th-anniversary celebration from the Royal Albert Hall in London, told me that without the programme choral music in Britain would be in an even more parlous state than he thinks it already is. He is worried by a dramatic fall over the last 15 years in boys and girls applying for places in cathedral choir schools. 'Actually for me, whether people watch in huge numbers or not is less important than the huge benefit the programme offers in bringing literally hundreds of thousands of people together, who find they enjoy singing together and, almost without noticing, learn from each other. It's a priceless artistic heritage.'

Michael Wakelin, who took over as series producer in 2001, believes that as well as including every sort of spiritually inspired music, the programme can 'sanctify' secular music. He gave the example of how a story of a drug addict who found faith was complemented on *Songs of Praise* from Belfast by a pop song. Her story was that her life was in a total mess. She was on the run from the police and was eventually caught and locked up. She carried her old auntie's Bible with her to her cell as a talisman, but never read it. One day, however, she opened it and found the passage in the first chapter of Isaiah

## MILLENNIUM CELEBRATIONS

*Songs of Praise*'s biggest ever programme came from Cardiff's Millennium Stadium on the first Sunday in 2000.

*Main picture*: Many choirs unite in praise.

*Left, bottom*: The crowd celebrates the new millennium with song.

*Below*: Sir Cliff Richard sings his 'Millennium Prayer'.

*Right, top*: Over 60,000 people pack the Millennium Stadium.

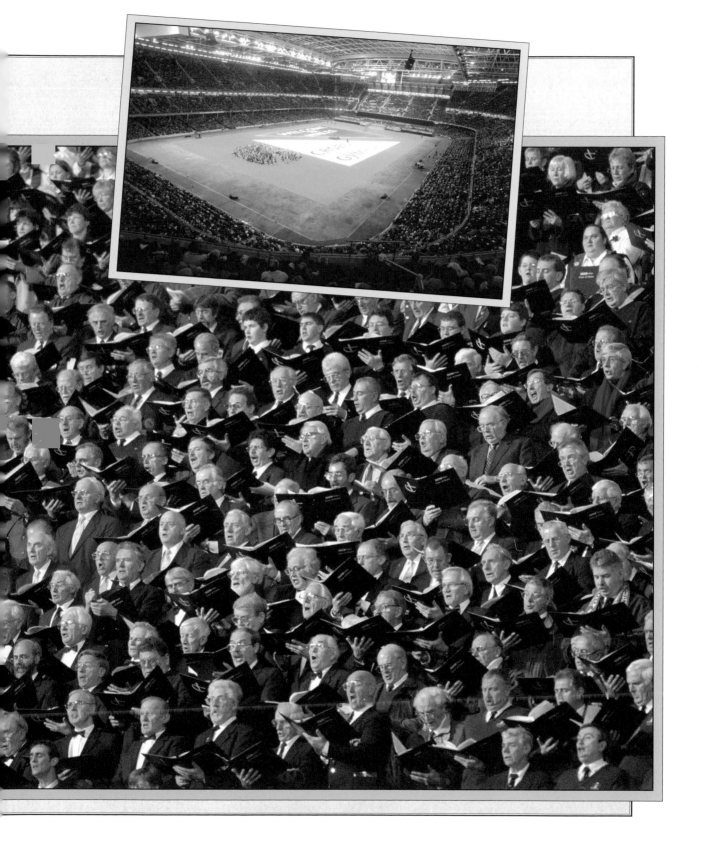

about being washed as white as snow. She was astonished. She said, 'I had expected to find judgment in the Bible, and here was mercy.' Michael followed this tale on the programme with Jimmy Ruffin singing 'I Can See Clearly Now'. It was a powerful moment.

He said, 'I have also featured Toyah singing Bette Midler's "The Rose" and Michael Ball singing the theme song from the film *Titanic*. These crossover songs have a part to play in the future of *Songs of Praise* as people with a knowledge of hymns become fewer. We need to play them the music that they know with lyrics that make sense for them in both a sacred and secular context.'

From the beginning, *Songs of Praise* developed close ties with its audience. Regular viewers have bonded with it and, as Hugh Faupel put it, the programme belongs to them. In the end it was the viewers, not the producers, who insisted that the words should be shown on the screen, a technical addition only possible in the latter part of the programme's life, but that will seem very small beer in times to come. We are in a new age of digital broadcasting. BBC Religion has its own website. However unlikely it may seem to those wrestling for the first time with a home computer or who still have difficulties with a remote-controlled television and video recorder, the possibilities created by these new items are almost limitless.

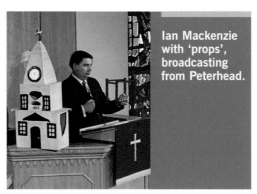

Ian Mackenzie with 'props', broadcasting from Peterhead.

How about being able to call up the history of your favourite hymn on one side of your TV screen, while it is being sung on the other? How about selecting your favourite moment from the programme with the click of a computer mouse and replaying it whenever you want? How about collecting and editing together all your favourite hymns in your own order and illustrating them with the pictures and images that make most sense to you? It is all possible. Britain's most switched-on computer-buffs, young teenagers, are already doing this with their pop music.

Whatever else can be said about *Songs of Praise*, it is a survivor. It has seen off or outlived rivals from *Stars on Sunday* to *Highway*. There have been many ingenious ideas for programmes to replace *Songs of Praise* but nothing has ever succeeded. No one dedicated more energy to the enterprise than another inventive Scot, Ian Mackenzie. Minister, broadcaster, film-maker and musician Ian's musical celebrations also asked awkward questions. In one such series, *What Shall We Do with the Abbey?*, he looked at the problems of Paisley Abbey at a time when costly repairs were needed. Frank Topping and the late Donald Swann began in the cold empty church and gradually conjured up more and more choristers of all ages, as well as the singer Garth Hewitt and the BBC Scottish Radio Orchestra, to join them. They would have raised the roof, if it had not been so unsafe.

Frank Topping and Gloria Hunniford took the professional risks of their lives in presenting *Dial-a-Hymn*, my own attempt to compete with *Songs of Praise* when I worked for ITV. *Dial-a-Hymn* went out live, and was similar to *Songs of Praise* with a large congregation of singers, but different in that viewers chose the hymns to be sung by telephoning the church directly. Frank and Gloria chatted to the people who got through about what tune they wanted and why they liked a particular hymn, while the conductor and organist feverishly looked the hymn up and quickly decided on descants and number of verses. Now that digital technology makes interaction between the television audience and a programme increasingly possible, I hope that *Songs of Praise* will try it out one day.

Meanwhile, viewers like Wallace Grevatt in Brighton, who never misses an edition and appears now and again in the ranks of singers himself, look forward to future developments. 'I always enjoy something new,' Wallace says, adding, 'I'd love to see some of the great programmes from the past again.'

I shall give my friend and former boss, Colin Morris – church leader, BBC controller, broadcaster and once a *Songs of Praise* presenter himself – the final word about the programme. In his address at the service of thanksgiving for 30 years of *Songs of Praise*, he summed up for me why the programme still appeals to something quite deep within us:

*Lastly, we are able to sing the Lord's song in a strange land because we are exiles, and it's the song of home – haunting us, teasing our memories, prodding us about our destiny. The basic condition of fallen humanity is homesickness, alienation from God, our neighbour and ourselves. The great early-church theologian Tertullian said, 'The soul is naturally Christian'. He was echoing Jesus' words, 'The kingdom of heaven is within you.' It's bred in our bone, part of our structure; we are born to believe; we resonate to the call of the kingdom*

*Right*: **The 2001 *Songs of Praise* team in their office 'home' in Manchester.**

*as a flower turns its face to the sun; the way a divining rod quivers in the presence of water in the desert.*

*It's all there in the parable of the prodigal son whose story could be summarized in three terse phrases – sick of home, homesick, home. That's the human saga and we are all somewhere along that path between the far country and home.*

*Songs of Praise articulates the poignancy of that journey which is inspired by crisis, undertaken in faith, beset by danger and accomplished in triumph. It gives melodies to march to and songs to cheer our spirits, and orchestrates our celebration when we arrive at our journey's end.*

# Selected *Songs of Praise* presenters and locations: 1961–2001

## Presenters

**A**

Kriss Akabusi
Juliet Alexander
Ronald Allison
Agnellus Andrew
Michael Armitage
Douglas Armstrong

**B**

Richard Baker
Sally Barnes
Michael Barratt
Martin Bashir
Michael Baughan
Raymond Baxter
David Bellamy
David Biddle
Dickie Bird
John L. Bird
Eric Blennerhassett
Edgar Boucher
Noreen Bray
Percy Brewster
Fiona Bruce
Michael Buerk

**C**

Donald Cairns
Dick Cameron
Christopher Campling
Jeremy Carrad
Steve Chalke
Bob Christie
Charlotte Church
John Cole
Tom Coyne
Andrew Cruickshank
Julian Cullingford
James Curry
Mark Curry

**D**

Lionel Dakers
Dana
Jill Dando
John Darran
David Davies
Colin Day
David Dimbleby
James Dow
Mary Downing
Robert Duncan
John Dunn

**E**

Barrie Edgar
Michael Elder
Reverend Noel Evans

**F**

Ronald Falconer
Jumoke Fashola
Howie Firth
Peter Firth

Tom Fleck
Tom Fleming
David Franklin

**G**

Ian Gall
Phil George
John Gibbs
Alan Gibson
P. Selvin Goldberg
Krishnan Guru-Murphy

**H**

Thomas Haliwell
Rosemary Hartill
Russell Harty
Thora Hird
Brian Hoey
Eamonn Holmes
George House
Robert Hudson
Dick Hughes
Stephanie Hughes
Gloria Hunniford

**J**

Bernard Jackson
Michael Jackson-Campbell
Emyr Jenkins
Aled Jones
Paul Jones
Diane-Louise Jordan

**K**

Kenneth Kendall
Anne Kirkbride
Douglas Kynoch

**H**

Philip Latham
Sue Lawley
Donald Leggat
Geoffrey Lewis

Martyn Lewis
Ronald Lloyd
Stuart Lochrie
Johnny Logan

**M**

Deborah McAndrew
Ian McCaskill
Paul McDowell
Patrick McEnroe
Seamus McKee
Kenneth McKellar
Bruce McKenzie
Keith Macklin
Don MacLean
Murdoch McPherson
Angus MacVicar
Ruth Madoc
Bill Magee
Magnus Magnusson
Sally Magnusson
M.R. Mainwaring
Christopher Martin-Jenkins
David Matthew
Michael Meech
Fritz Mehntens
Cliff Michelmore
Gerry Monte
Kieron Moore
Cliff Morgan
Colin Morris
Martin Muncaster
Denis Murray

**N**

William Neil
John Neville
Roy Noble

**O**

Daniel O'Donnell
James O'Hara

**P**

Nick Page
Bruce Parker
David Parry-Jones
Glyn Parry-Jones
Leonard Pearcey
Margaret Percy
Ian Pitt-Watson
Simon Preston
William Purcell
Graham Purches

**R**

Lincoln Ralphs
Harry Rann
Gordon Reynolds
Pam Rhodes
Cliff Richard
Gwilym ap Robert
John Stuart Roberts
Michael Rodd
Chris Rogers
Roger Royle

**S**

Isla St Clair
Tom Salmon
Henry Sandon
Dudley Savage
Jimmy Saville
Hugh Scully
Harry Secombe
Colin Semper
Raymond Short
Leonard Small
Delia Smith
Howard Souster
David Steel
Moira Stewart

**T**

Cyril Taylor
Gwynfryn Thomas
Debbie Thrower

Leslie Timmins
John Timpson
Alan Titchmarsh
Ruby Turner

**V**

Ian Valentine

**W**

Eddie Waring
David Watson
Joy Webb
Pauline Webb
Peter West
Geoffrey Wheeler
Willard White
Toyah Wilcox
David Willcocks
Austen Williams
Ifan Wyn Williams
Kevin Woodford
Mike Woodridge

# Locations

**A**

Aberdeen
Aberdovey
Aberfan
Accrington
Aldershot
Alfriston
Algarve
Alnwick
Alton Towers
Ambleside
Ambridge
Atlanta
Ayr

**B**

*Ballykissangel*
Barnsley
Beaumaris

Beckenham
Belfast
Benidorm
Berlin
Bolsover
Bracknell
Bradford
Bridgenorth
Bristol
Brixton
Broadmoor
Budleigh Salterton
Bunbury

**C**

Campbeltown
Canterbury
Cardiff
Carrick Fergus
Channel Tunnel
Chatteris
Clogher
*Coronation Street*
Corrymeela
Costa del Sol
Coventry
Coverack

**D**

Dagenham
Dedham
Detroit
Dresden
Dordoigne
Downpatrick
Dulwich
Dunblane
Dunkirk

**E**

Ealing
East Kilbride
East Neuk of Fife
Eastbourne

Ebbw Vale
Eccles
Eden Project
Ely
Eton College
Euston

**F**

Faversham
Festival Hall
Fishguard
Florida
Folkestone
Fountains Abbey
Fraserburgh
Frome

**G**

Glasgow
Glastonbury
Glossop
Goring and Streatley
Goudhurst
Greenock
Grimsby
Guernsey
Guildford

**H**

Hackney
*Heartbeat*
Heathrow
Henley
Hexham
Hitchin
Holmfirth
Hong Kong
Howden Minster

**I**

Ilford
Ilfracombe
Innellan
Iona

Ipswich
Isle of Dogs
Isle of Man
Islington

**J**
Jarrow
Jedburgh
Jersey
Jerusalem
Johannesburg

**K**
Keithley
Kendal
Kilburn
Kilmarnock
Kingston, Jamaica
Kirby Lonsdale
Kirk Yetholm
Knighton

**L**
Lake of Galilee
*Last of the Summer
   Wine*
Leeds
Leeds Castle
Leek
Leighton Buzzard
Lincoln
Llanelli
Lourdes
Louth
Lowestoft
Luton
Lyme Regis

**M**
Majorca
Mallaig
Mayfield
Melbourne
Melrose

Morriston
Moscow
Mousehole
Mytholmroyd

**N**
Nantwich
Nashville
Newbury
Newcastle
Northwood
Norwich
Nottingham

**P**
Padstow
Paris
Peel
Peterhead
Pin Green
Port Stanley
Portrush
Prague
Purley

**Q**
QPR football ground

**R**
Randalstown
Reading
Redruth
Rhosllanerchrugog
Ripon
Rome
Royal Albert Hall
Rugby
Rye

**S**
St Keverne
St Neots
Scarborough
Scilly Isles

Shanghai
Sherbourne
Southall
Southend-on-Sea
Southwell Minster
Stanstead Airport
Steyning
Stratford-upon-Avon
Swansea
Sydney

**T**
Taizé
Takapuna
Tenby
Tenerife
Todmorden
Tonga
Tooting
Trondheim
Truro

**U**
Uppingham

**V**
Vale of Aylesbury
Valletta
Vancouver
Vienna

**W**
Wakefield
Walmer
Warwick
Wells
Welshpool
Wembley
Weston-super-Mare
Whitby
Witney
Wokingham
Worcester
Wormwood Scrubs

Worth Valley Railway

**Y**
Yeovil
York

**Z**
Zimbabwe